RELAPSE
TRAPS

RELAPSE TRAPS

HOW TO AVOID THE 12 MOST COMMON PITFALLS IN RECOVERY

Ronald L. Rogers
and
Chandler Scott McMillin

Foreword by James R. Milam, Ph.D.

Produced by The Philip Lief Group, Inc.

Bantam Books
New York Toronto London Sydney Auckland

RELAPSE TRAPS

A Bantam Book / January 1992

The Twelve Steps are reprinted with permission of Alcoholics Anonymous
World Services, Inc. Permission to reprint the Twelve Steps does not mean
that AA has reviewed or approved the contents of this publication, nor that
AA agrees with the views expressed herein. AA is a program of recovery
from alcoholism—use of the Twelve Steps in connection with programs
and activities which are patterned after AA, but which address other
problems, does not imply otherwise.
Quotes on pages 61 and 79 are reprinted with permission of
AA World Services, Inc.

Library of Congress Cataloging-in-Publication Data

Rogers, Ronald.
Relapse traps : how to avoid the 12 most common pitfalls in
recovery / Ronald L. Rogers and Chandler Scott McMillin; foreword
by James R. Milam.
p.   cm.
Includes bibliographical references.
ISBN 0-553-35479-5
1. Alcoholics—Rehabilitation.   2. Alcoholism—Relapse—
Prevention.   3. Narcotic addicts—Rehabilitation.   4. Drug abuse—
Relapse—Prevention.   I. McMillin, Chandler.   II. Title.
HV5276.R65   1992
616.86'106—dc20   91-22613
                                                      CIP

Published simultaneously in the United States and Canada

Bantam Books are published by Bantam Books, a division of Bantam Doubleday Dell Publishing Group, Inc. Its trademark, consisting of the words
"Bantam Books" and the portrayal of a rooster, is Registered in U.S. Patent
and Trademark Office and in other countries. Marca Registrada. Bantam
Books, 666 Fifth Avenue, New York, New York 10103.

PRINTED IN THE UNITED STATES OF AMERICA

BVG   0 9 8 7 6 5 4 3 2 1

DEDICATION

This book is dedicated to the thousands of alcoholics and addicts we have known and worked with over the past two decades. We have learned from their experience, their strength, their hope, and in some cases, sadly, their deaths. Some of their names are listed below. We apologize to the many we left out.

No one contributes more to the understanding of a disease than its victims, and no one ever had better teachers than we did. This book is to honor you.

Jack A.	Walking Bob	Phil F.
Bunky H.	Warren K.	Baltimore Bill
Jim H.	Tommy T.	Tank
Jim S.	Vicki M.	Beth K.
Dale M.	Kathy T.	Clyde H.
Herb W.	Joe Q.	Betty O.
June W.	Ken B.	Bobby Z.
Mac M.	Doug G.	Patty K.
Dicky S.	Frankie S.	Jimmy F.
Jim P.	Karen D.	Chris P.
Jim M.	Jane M.	Andrea H.
Ruby G.	Eric	Jan K.
Lamont L.	Clint R.	Bob F.
Toni L.	Harold S.	Bill L.
Gene R.	Ed S.	Chris C.
Jim G.	Don B.	Johnny J.
LaVera G.	Jack L.	Jean M.
Blind Al	Eileen B.	Clint D.

Walter C.	John S.	Bev S.
Jack R.	Lee M.	Samms S.
John R.	Rich A.	Bob E.
Benny C.	Harvey B.	Don K.
Sandy B.	Hambone	Mel S.
Lee S.	Linda D.	Jim M.
Dennis "Captain V"	Calvin P.	Lee H.
Joe M.	Jimmy G.	Andy M.

CONTENTS

FOREWORD

In over twenty years of treating alcoholics and other addicts I have encountered many patients who have relapsed after prior treatments. Reasons given are often stressful life experiences—loss of a job, a divorce, a financial crisis, or a spell of depression. Thus sobriety is viewed as being dependent on the ability to avoid or to cope with these troublesome experiences. I reject all such reasons for relapse as mere excuses, because all relapses I have seen have always revealed a prior weakness or lapse in the patient's sobriety maintenance program.

I have developed a formula that explains all relapses in this light. I regularly share the formula with patients somewhat as follows:

"If you are wondering if you are going to relapse in the future, I will give you the answer now. There are two parts to the answer, so don't panic when you hear the first half. If you are addicted, of course you are going back to alcohol or drugs. That is part of the meaning of addiction. Your addiction doesn't need help with 'causes' of relapse. It will handle the job alone, as quickly when you don't have problems (complacency) as when you do. Now the other half, the full statement. Of course you will relapse, unless you are protected. Sobriety maintenance is preventive maintenance. The protection has to be in place before you need it. If you are fully protected within your program of living sober, nothing can cause you to relapse."

McMillin and Rogers have provided the much-needed shift in focus from life problems to protection priorities. Environmental stresses don't cause addiction; learning to cope with them won't prevent relapse.

Of course, all relapse prevention starts with competent treatment in the first place. The treatment must provide a thorough understanding of addictive disease and what is required for recovery. It empowers the individual, not to fight the addiction directly, which he can't, but to learn and to live by the principles that prevent the addiction from asserting control.

Within this essential orientation, the authors are most helpful by being very specific. They identify and explain the common mistakes and weaknesses in sobriety maintenance that allow the addiction to assert itself and cause relapse. In the process they greatly strengthen the understanding of both the disease and the recovery process.

I highly recommend this book both for treatment staffs and for all patients recovering from addictive disease.

—James R. Milam, Ph.D.
Author of *Under the Influence*

RELAPSE
TRAPS

INTRODUCTION

This is a book about relapse and how to avoid it.

We began working with addicts and alcoholics about twenty years ago, and it was clear to us from the beginning that relapse was the central obstacle to recovery. If an alcoholic could maintain abstinence, he could probably handle any of the other problems that might come up, but if he couldn't stay away from alcohol and drugs, then very little else would change for the better.

Thus we, like everyone else in the addiction field, set out to discover the secret of relapse. What was it that led certain of our patients to return to alcohol and drug use in spite of the tragedy it wrought? What caused otherwise intelligent human beings to sacrifice careers, families, their own lives, and often those of their loved ones, in the pursuit of something that came in a bottle, a needle, a tablet, or a pipe? While others sought the key to success, we wanted to know: *What is the secret of failure?*

As usual, there was no shortage of answers. Psychoanalysts blamed relapse on an "addictive personality," which they claimed poisoned the addict's thinking even after months or years of sobriety. Family therapists saw it as a symptom of disturbed relationships. The clergy spoke of spiritual bankruptcy, while scientists believed the answer lay in developing "safe" drugs to substitute for those on which the addict had come to depend. Educators emphasized the importance of self-esteem and job training, while social scientists proclaimed the need to eliminate racism, poverty, and injustice. Within Alcoholics Anonymous and the other Twelve Step fellowships, relapse was seen as proof positive that the disease was "cunning, baffling, and powerful."

In this respect, no one was more baffled than the relapsers themselves. (Note: Throughout this book, not only the names but also any personal characteristics that could help to identify the subject of a case history or the source of a quote have been changed.) "I have all the right intentions," one mourned, "but then things don't go the way I want, and before I know it, I'm drinking again."

"For me, it's stress," complained another. "I let myself get upset about something, and then I can't sleep and I can't relax, and pretty soon I'm thinking about getting loaded."

"I can handle stress," one woman insisted, "but I go absolutely nuts when I don't have anything to do. When I'm bored, that's when I get a real craving."

"My last binge was after a fight with my girlfriend," someone else offered. "I feel that no matter what I do, it isn't good enough. I get to the point where I just figure, *what the hell?*"

"My problem is that I'm more depressed sober than when I was on drugs," said another. "I can't seem to shake it. The only thing that helps is a drug."

The number and variety of situations that seemed to trigger relapse were overwhelming, and we looked to put them in some semblance of order. As we did, several things became clear.

First and foremost, *people relapsed for different reasons.* In fact, people often relapsed for different reasons at different points in their lives. The problem that got someone drunk after twelve weeks of being sober was not necessarily the one that provoked a relapse after six months or two years of abstinence.

Second, although relapse could occur at any time in the addict's recovery, *it was particularly common in the first year.* In fact, the longer the addict was able to remain abstinent, the greater the chance that abstinence would develop into stable, long-term sobriety.

Third, we came to believe that relapse was rooted less in emotional instability than in attitude and behavior. This is contrary to popular wisdom. Most people assume that relapse is always precipitated by some type of crisis and is, in fact, a response to intense, painful feelings with which the relapser cannot cope. Not so. In the majority of cases, relapse is the product of a series of bad decisions, each one based on the one that preceded it, until a return to alcohol or drugs seems to be the only "reasonable" choice.

We decided to reverse the cart and horse. Instead of viewing relapse as the result of emotional problems, we began to see it as *a mistake in judgment surrounded* (and often obscured) *by strong emotions.*

We came to understand that despite obvious differences in character and situation, most recovering people are faced with certain key choices, imposed by the nature of the disease itself. They respond in different ways to the demands of their illness— and therein lies the difference between "success" and "failure." If alcoholics and addicts could develop attitudes and behaviors that reflected the reality of life with an addictive disease, relapse could be virtually eliminated. They would still face problems, but relapse would no longer be foremost among them, and it has long been our belief that a sober addict or alcoholic is capable of handling almost anything.

Fourth, we decided that the common precipitants of relapse could be grouped into twelve broad categories, then studied with an eye to developing strategies for avoiding a return to alcohol and drugs. These twelve categories became the basis for the "relapse traps" we explore in this book.

Last, and perhaps most important, we realized that relapse wasn't confined to addiction. It is in fact a problem that afflicts the treatment of many diseases, including most of our biggest killers—cancer, heart disease, and diabetes. By thinking of relapse as *a human and medical problem* rather than a sign of psychological abnormality, we see that the addict and alcoholic are not so different from the heart patient, the cancer victim, the diabetic. Each struggles to accommodate the demands and limitations imposed by chronic disease. Naturally, some patients struggle more than others.

It is our experience that no matter how complex the alcoholic or addict's personality, the causes of relapse are fairly straightforward. So are its ultimate solutions. Once we understand the nature of recovery, the various risks are laid out before our feet like traps along a jungle trail. They're only dangerous if you can't see them, or if you fail to take the necessary steps to avoid them. Like those of the jungle, the traps of relapse can be baited to seem quite seductive.

The phenomenon of relapse has led many people—addicts, alcoholics, families, even professionals—to conclude that treatment is hopeless. Nothing could be further from the truth. The evidence is all around you. At this point in time there are probably more than a million recovering people in the various Twelve Step fellowships, with new members being added every day. As you read this, there's probably a meeting going on somewhere, not far from where you live. And remember you are not alone: some of them slipped along the way, sometimes more than once. Somehow, they found a way to put an end to relapse and to establish stable sobriety. They are living proof that relapse can be overcome.

Our intention is to show you how they did it, and how you can, too. We'll cover issues like these:

1. how people recover
2. why some people relapse and others don't
3. why relapsers are blind to relapse until it's too late
4. how to assess your own risk for relapse at various points in your recovery
5. how to reduce your risk of relapse by changing certain key behaviors
6. how to develop a recovery program strong enough to minimize the possibility of relapse
7. how other people can help you avoid relapse
8. how to recognize the thinking processes that usually precede relapse

As we proceed, we'll also focus on the family. We'll talk about how concerned persons can interrupt a relapse already under way. To supplement our advice, we've provided a Suggested Reading section that lists publications that expand on the themes of this book.

Ready? Let's begin with the obvious: What is a relapse?

PART ONE:
THE
ANATOMY
OF
RECOVERY

WHAT IS RELAPSE?

To define relapse, we must first define addiction. And that isn't as simple as it sounds. In fact, there are dozens of definitions currently in use.

The various forms of drug dependency—on alcohol, cocaine, heroin, et cetera—are subcategories of *addictive disease*. This is a grouping of related disorders in much the same way that "heart disease" represents a number of cardiological conditions. Despite their obvious differences, all forms of addictive disease share certain key features. They're *chronic,* meaning they last a long time. They are *progressive,* meaning they worsen over time, with one complication often leading to the next. They are *primary* disorders, meaning they possess their own etiology, symptoms, and course, and can therefore be separated from coexisting problems such as depression or bipolar disorder. All addictions are potentially fatal—they directly or indirectly decrease the life expectancy of their victims.

Addictive disease can be recognized by physiological and behavioral symptoms. *Tolerance* is the ability to consume larger than normal amounts of a drug without showing some of the signs of intoxication. *Physical dependence* is indicated by the appearance of withdrawal symptoms when the drug is removed from the system. *Pathological organ change* means there is evidence of actual physical damage as a result of repeated doses of the drug.

Behaviorally, addicts normally experience *compulsion,* which causes them to consume more of the drug than they originally intended. *Loss of control* indicates that the user has trouble confining his consumption to predetermined amount, times, or locations—or, in some cases, has extreme difficulty terminating an episode of drug use. *Continued use despite adverse consequences* implies that the addict repeatedly returns to the drug despite the problems it causes.

Behavioral symptoms are more common than physical symptoms, and this creates some confusion. For example, many disorders feature compulsion—compulsive gambling and compulsive overeating being two examples—but do not include the physiological symptoms characteristic of alcoholism and drug dependence such as tolerance and physical withdrawal. For clarity's sake, we should probably describe gambling and overeating as compulsive disorders rather than as forms of addictive disease. Though there are similarities between these conditions and alcoholism, there are also key differences—not the least of which is long-term, heavy exposure to a toxic substance.

WHAT IS TREATMENT?

Though we have no cure for addictive disease, we do possess an effective method for arresting its course: abstinence. Alcoholism and drug addiction can only kill during the active, dangerous phase, when the alcoholic or addict is exposing himself to the twin dangers of intoxication and withdrawal. Thus the baseline treatment for all addictions is the same: stop using the drug.

Treatment programs, in this respect, are supports for abstinence. Alcoholics Anonymous and other Anonymous groups support abstinence by providing a sober peer group and a program of spiritual growth. Detoxification units support abstinence by helping to manage withdrawal symptoms. Rehabilitation programs support abstinence through individual and group counseling. But no matter how complex these programs become, the goal of treatment never changes.

In this respect, programs such as methadone maintenance are not treatment at all, because they don't include abstinence. They are designed to control drug-taking behavior rather than to treat addiction. The patient on methadone maintenance is just as addicted as he was when using heroin.

WHAT IS RELAPSE?

Relapse, therefore, is best defined as a return to drinking or drugs after an intervening period of abstinence. Because the definition doesn't specify the length of the abstinent period or of the return to drug use, relapses may be frequent or rare, brief or prolonged. Some experts feel relapse should include only those persons who have completed formal treatment and then returned to drugs. But many alcoholics and addicts stop drinking and using drugs for extended periods without the benefit of formal treatment.

Still other experts have maintained that relapse should be confined to those persons for whom a return to drinking or drugs has been accompanied by clear signs of loss of control. Again, we believe that for the addict loss of control is inevitable, once drinking or drugging has been reintroduced. Why wait for indisputable evidence of something you already know is only a matter of time? And some authors feel we should date relapse from the first signs of a return to old ways of thinking and acting—in some cases, months before the recovering alcoholic picks up the first drink. But most if not all addicts experience at least some periods of emotional and behavioral "regression" during the process of recovery without actually returning to drugs. Thus, we feel it is misleading to classify that as relapse.

As long as you remember that the baseline treatment for addictive disease—the action that renders its victim safe from death and harm—is abstinence, and that relapse is a return to drinking or drug use following abstinence, no matter what the reason, you can't go wrong.

Now that we've defined relapse, let's take a look at its significance in terms of recovery.

HOW PEOPLE FAIL

Most people assume that relapse is a sign that treatment has failed. But we think that's a simplistic view. An alcoholic or addict who relapses may eventually—perhaps quite soon—give up alcohol and drugs again. Many of the counselors working in treatment programs around the nation would at one point have qualified as "treatment failures" by the criteria they apply to their own patients. They, like many of the founders of Alcoholics Anonymous, suffered one or more relapses during the struggle for sobriety.

It makes us wonder about the validity of short-term outcome studies in general. Just a few weeks ago we were guests on a television show along with a 19-year-old recovering addict who was being portrayed to the viewers as an example of successful treatment. He had been drug-free for over a year. But as we waited for the show to begin, he explained that his last and ultimately "successful" treatment was really his fourth.

His first experience had been in an outpatient program. "I wasn't ready," he admitted. "I didn't make much of an effort. I chipped around with drugs all through the program and finally dropped out." The second attempt was at an inpatient facility. "That time, I really wanted to succeed, but it was no use. I got loaded the day I left." His third treatment was for six months at a long-term facility in another state. Once again, he responded well while in the program and stayed clean for several months after returning home. After yet another painful relapse, he entered a second outpatient program—and was able to remain sober.

This patient no doubt appears to be a "treatment failure" in the records of the first three programs and a "success" in those of the last. But from his perspective, each treatment had been extremely important in his ultimate recovery. The effects of counseling, education, and Twelve Step participation seemed in his case to be cumulative. Recovery included a succession of errors in judgment and decision making, from which he learned important lessons about his own limitations and the restrictions imposed by his disease.

As he put it: "I began to realize that I was my own worst enemy. Not only did I make mistakes, I would make the same ones over and over again."

If this same young man was to get drunk tomorrow, would we reclassify him as a failure?

Again, we think this problem stems in part from our national preoccupation with short-term rather than long-term results. Everyone knows that a number of patients relapse following treatment. But this obviously doesn't mean (as the above example illustrates) that they are barred from success at some future point. What happens to addicts and alcoholics five or ten years after they've completed a treatment program? This is an area in which relatively few studies have been done.

The reason for the paucity of research is fairly simple: it's hard to follow alcoholics and addicts for an extended period. Most people find this difficult to understand. "What's the big deal?" they insist. "You keep in touch with the addicts for five or ten years after they leave your program, and see if they go back to drugs. It's a piece of cake."

But of course, it isn't. Tracking addicts and alcoholics isn't as simple as staying in touch with your cousin. Addicts frequently change addresses, relocate to new cities, start new careers or businesses, marry or divorce—in most cases leaving very little in the way of a paper trail. Their confidentiality must be strictly protected; some have not told new employers or landlords about their history. Any large-scale effort to monitor outcome usually requires a full-time tracing department and outside funding. Even then it's likely your data will fall under the heading "Lost Contact."

As a result, most follow-up studies confine themselves to the period from six months to two years following treatment. Some of these studies have concluded that treatment succeeds at a rate of only 25% to 35%, and that most addicts and alcoholics experience continued problems including multiple hospitalization, declining economic and social welfare, incarceration, and death. The rare long-term study seemed to indicate similar results over the five- to ten-year period following treatment. One study from Sweden found that 52% of patients were either dead or required constant supervision.

But other studies have indicated that the prognosis for the typical American alcoholic isn't anywhere near that grim. A ten-year follow-up of two hundred patients selected at random from a population completing treatment at a hospital in Georgia found that 61% reported complete or stable remission for at least three years prior to the survey, and 84% reported "stable psychosocial status"—meaning their lives were obviously *not* the chaos portrayed by other studies. The survey showed that 76% were sober at the ten-year mark; of those who had died,

23% had been abstinent at death. The principal predictor of recovery turned out to be (as other studies have suggested) involvement in Alcoholics Anonymous. Alcoholics who not only went to meetings but sponsored others were sober at a rate of 91% ten years following treatment.

Quite a change from the picture normally presented to the public, isn't it? Perhaps the natural history of recovery for many addicts *includes* the experience of relapse. Obviously, relapse— though dangerous—is not a very good indicator of ultimate failure.

Relapse does, however, correlate strongly with danger and death. The fellowships of Alcoholics, Narcotics, and Cocaine Anonymous are replete with stories of people who "fell off the wagon" only to pay the ultimate price: that of life itself. Their deaths prove that relapse should be seen as a learning experience of the most dangerous sort. That's the purpose of this book—to use the hard lessons of your predecessors in recovery as a guide to a better, more stable kind of sobriety.

But first, the basics. Having examined recovery in general, let's personalize our discussion by looking at the best way to establish a program of recovery for yourself.

THREE KEYS
TO THE DOOR
OF RECOVERY

THE FIRST KEY:
_____ DEVELOP A FEEDBACK SYSTEM _____

One of the most overworked terms in treatment is *support system.* Counselors constantly urge their patients to develop one. The patients nod sagely and appear to take this to heart. Yet one day we happened to overhear the following interaction between two patients in our treatment center.

REGGIE: So look, have you got a support system for when you leave the program?

BUD: Yeah, sure. Well, I think so. What exactly is it?

REGGIE: You know, how you're going to get your support when you're out there on your own. Like, who is gonna keep you sober?

BUD: I thought I was.

REGGIE: You are, but who is gonna help you? Like AA or something.

BUD: How about my wife? She's already supporting me.

The fact is, many of our patients—and the counselors who treat them—have no idea what a support system is supposed to provide, which makes it nearly impossible to develop one.

Here are four things that should characterize your support system:

1. *It should be there when you need it.* A good support system needs to be available. That doesn't mean that people drop everything when you call. It does mean you should be able to reach someone on the telephone within a reasonable period.

2. *It should involve more than one person.* If you're going to depend on a support system, you want to spread your dependence around so that it doesn't become a burden to any one person. If you sense you're taxing someone's time and energy, you'll probably stop calling—which defeats the purpose.

3. *It should provide* emotional *but not financial support.* You need to learn to take care of yourself financially. Even if you're in a halfway house trying to save enough money to get out on your own, you should contribute something to your own upkeep.

4. *It should provide you with accurate feedback about your behavior and your attitudes.* This is perhaps most important. You need the feedback of others because your own thinking is probably influenced by defense mechanisms. Even if their feedback is sometimes inaccurate, you should always seek it out. Discuss your decisions with your support system before you put them into action.

For most recovering people, the support system is culled from within a Twelve Step group. Notice we said "from"—every AA member dealing with an alcohol problem and NA member handling a drug problem develops a set of close friends and associates within his/her particular fellowship (AA for recovery from alcoholism, and NA, CA, etc. for problems with other drugs) rather than trying to relate to the fellowship as a whole.

WHAT'S A SPONSOR, AND HOW DO YOU CHOOSE ONE?

A sponsor is a guide, a confidant, an instructor in recovery the Twelve Step way. Theoretically, the sponsor benefits from the relationship as much as the newcomer or "pigeon," because, as the slogan says, the best way to keep your sobriety is to give it away to someone else.

Look for the following qualities in a sponsor:

1. Availability. Once again, all the wisdom in the world is useless if you can't reach someone to find out what they think.

2. They know how to stay sober. As demonstrated by their success. Don't pick somebody who doesn't have a stable recovery of their own, no matter how much you may like them. Those people can be friends, but they shouldn't be sponsors.

3. They're willing to be honest with you. In other words, they demonstrate the nerve to tell you when you're full of it. This is without a doubt the single most valuable commodity in your recovery. At some point, you are going to need this more than anything else. Many perfectly nice, caring, warm, intelligent people simply cannot bring themselves to do this. Don't select them for your sponsor.

CAN GROUP THERAPY BE PART OF A SUPPORT SYSTEM?

Group therapy—led by a counselor or other professional— should be considered treatment rather than support. Of course, some groups confuse the two tasks. The purpose of treatment is to accomplish four goals:

1. to increase your knowledge of addiction
2. to help you *self-diagnose*—that is, recognize that you have an addictive disease
3. to introduce and facilitate your involvement in effective programs for ongoing recovery
4. to help you take personal responsibility for maintaining your program

Support, on the other hand, can include comfort, sympathy, healing—all of which you will probably need on the long road to recovery.

Problems occur when you try to mix the structured tasks of treatment with the more nebulous function of support. When the two are confused, group therapy may actually become part of the relapse cycle. One woman complained that her husband (having been drinking off and on for the past year following nine sober months) claimed he was in treatment despite his relapses because he still attended weekly outpatient group sessions with a local psychiatrist. His reason: he was hoping to "motivate" himself to stop drinking. Of course, it failed. Attending this group was simply a way of preventing his wife from divorcing him. When she criticized his binges, he countered with the argument that he was seeking help—was it his fault it wasn't working? It was a clever ruse to disguise the reality that treatment begins with abstinence.

THE SECOND KEY: USING THE TWELVE STEPS

The Steps are designed to take you from an admission of powerlessness and unmanageability through a commitment to carry a message to those who still suffer. This is an enormous undertaking, and it's important to recall that for all their power, the Steps are nothing but *suggestions*.

USING THE STEPS IN DIFFERENT WAYS

Different people deal with problems differently at different stages in recovery. For example, the Third Step suggests you turn your will over to a Higher Power. Suppose you've been sober for six months, and you want to go on a trip to a convention in Borneo where all your peers are going to get drunk. Your sponsor tells you not to go, and you follow this advice. *I promised to turn my will over*, you remind yourself.

Three years later, your son, whom you've been trying to get into a drug program, is arrested for selling drugs and calls you to bail him out of jail in the middle of the night. You ask him if he's willing to go to the program, and he tells you he'd rather die first. Despite your fears of what might happen, you decide to leave him in jail. You turn your anxiety—and the outcome of your decision—over to your Higher Power.

The same Step was used in two vastly dissimilar situations. That's the essence of the Steps, and the source of their usefulness. As you change, so do they.

THE FIRST THREE STEPS ARE THE KEY

From an AA perspective, the key to recovery, and therefore to most relapse, is contained in the initial three Steps.

The First Step reads: "We admitted we were powerless over alcohol—that our lives had become unmanageable." This is the source of motivation for recovery. No one will treat a problem until he acknowledges its existence. Remember, the addict is probably the *last* person to grasp the extent and severity of his addiction. Everyone knows how desperately he has been affected except the alcoholic himself. The First Step is the remedy.

The Second Step suggests that the alcoholic look for a source of strength and hope outside himself. It reads, "Came to believe that a Power greater than ourselves could restore us to sanity." The addict is a classic example of *false independence*—

stubborn insistence on the right to make an endless number of bad decisions while under the influence of powerful toxins—so this Step is a direct instruction to abandon any hope of lasting recovery unless you have help.

In the Third Step, the addict is asked to turn his will and his life over to God—but a very special God. "Made a decision to turn our will and our lives over to the care of God as we understood Him." Twelve Step groups don't presume to interpret God for their members. They simply suggest that you find a Higher Power which works for you, and make use of it in your everyday life.

These Steps become the foundation for an enduring recovery. And where relapse occurs, the sponsor usually sends the relapser back to the first three Steps to search for the answer.

THE THIRD KEY:
UNDERSTANDING THE MEANING
OF UNCONDITIONAL
ABSTINENCE

Actually, this is incredibly simple. Unconditional means you don't drink or use drugs, no matter what.

Still, this causes confusion for addicts, whose thinking during their active addiction was dominated by conditions of all sorts, most of which led directly to more drug use. So they reflexively look for a situation in which relapse is *unavoidable*.

"Suppose I'm driving through the Mohave Desert," one alcoholic once asked us, "and my Jeep breaks down. And I check the canteen and it's empty. And the hours pass and I get thirstier and thirstier, and then the days pass and I'm dying of thirst. And then I discover under the spare tire this one last can of hot beer, which somebody left there months ago. And I look at that beer and think, 'This could save my life.' Are you telling me I can't drink it?"

"Listen," we advised, "if you're willing to go to all that trouble just to get yourself in a position where you absolutely have to drink a beer, then go right ahead. It's okay with us."

More than anything else, unconditional abstinence means dealing with the problems that occur during the course of recovery without resorting to that old standby, whether alcohol or drugs. Problems, then, are obstacles to be overcome rather than excuses to relapse.

So there are the three keys: develop a feedback system, practice the Twelve Steps, and make your abstinence unconditional. If you do that, you'll succeed—no matter how many obstacles are in your way.

Speaking of obstacles to sobriety, let's take a look at two of the most common: emotional upsets and the phenomenon of craving.

THE PROBLEM
OF EMOTIONS

Therapists constantly emphasize the importance of learning to deal with your emotions. But the recovering person experiences something quite out of the ordinary. We use Dr. Milam's term *emotional augmentation:* a brain syndrome characterized by overreaction to normal stress.

We're all familiar with periods when our emotions seem heightened. When we fall in love, for example. When we undergo a dramatic change in our lives: relocation, a job change, the birth of a child, divorce. During such periods we find ourselves overresponding to small irritations, perhaps saying or doing things we later regret.

Frequently, the roots of heightened emotionalism are physiological. We're all more sensitive to things when we're sick. Women—biologically more complex than males—are intimately familiar with periods of augmented emotion. For some, it's associated with the menstrual clock. Most experience it during pregnancy or following childbirth.

Recovery from addictive disease likewise represents a period of remarkable physical change. It's a bit like a second adolescence. The recovering person's body is something of a biochemical volcano—erupting from time to time in strange ways, shaping and influencing responses to ordinary events. A recovering person's ability to experience "serenity" is directly related to his or her success in dealing with augmented emotions.

Let's briefly look at some ways of coping with this type of emotionalism.

HOW TO LIVE WITH YOUR EMOTIONS

Having augmented emotions means you must take special care to avoid certain patterns of thinking that can drive you into a frenzy of anger or depression. They may seem quite justified at the time—maybe you really were treated unfairly, for example—but the end result will be intolerable, so we suggest the following three-step method.

1. STEP BACK FROM YOUR FEELINGS

When your emotions run high, they tend to dominate the rest of your personality. You not only feel different, you think and act differently as well. Recall the first time you fell in love. Didn't your friends think you were behaving strangely? Didn't you sometimes feel as though your rational faculties had gone into the deep freeze?

Neuroscientists sometimes say that the brain acts not as one but as three biological "computers": one ruling intellect, another instinct, a third emotion. Normally integrated, these functions sometimes conflict—especially when the "emotional computer" is in charge.

An example: suppose you're sitting in a restaurant, eating your lunch and thinking about your afternoon schedule. Your emotions are quiet, but your intellect is quite busy even as you eat, planning out your activities and making mental notes about each scheduled event. Suddenly, into the restaurant walks someone with whom you were madly in love and who dumped you. Before you know it, everything is forgotten in the wake of a flood of emotions. You stop eating—in fact, the food in your mouth suddenly tastes sour. Your stomach is invaded by a horde of butterflies. Your face is flushed, your forehead beaded with sweat. You can hear your heart pounding in your ears.

You're experiencing a *fight-or-flight* response, not unlike what grips an animal challenged by an enemy or frozen by the headlights of an oncoming truck. It's uncomfortable, to say the least.

Imagine that this person disappears into another room, giving you a chance to escape unseen. You immediately take advantage. A couple minutes later, you're walking down the street toward your car, still recovering from the shock of seeing your ex-lover. Gradually, your heart slows and your body returns to normal. Soon enough, you're wondering at the intensity of your own reaction. *I can't understand it,* you tell yourself. *You'd think we broke up yesterday. I thought I was over it.*

A few minutes afterward, you're once again thinking about your next appointment, the incident shoved into a corner of your mind for later consideration. By nightfall, it will seem remote, almost imaginary.

What you experienced was a temporary "argument" between your intellect and your emotions. Afflicted with a feeling of panic, you quickly found a remedy: (a) you left the stressful situation as soon as possible, and (b) you began "talking yourself down" from the heights of your anxiety, by reminding yourself that in fact, no real physical threat was posed. The fight-or-flight reaction you experienced was based on a relationship that was long dead.

That's also the best method for dealing with the augmented emotions that characterize recovery. Through experience, you learn to avoid basing your response on your initial "gut feeling." You automatically question whether the present situation merits intense feelings. The stronger your emotions, the more extensively you examine them before you take action.

The rationale? If you act on emotions artificially augmented by underlying physiological processes, you risk saying and doing something inappropriate to the situation. If there's anything wrong with your interpretation of a situation, and you don't check the validity of that interpretation before acting, you can find yourself in some embarrassing situations. Unless you are totally comfortable with apologizing all the time, we suggest you find an alternative.

2. EXAMINE THE VALIDITY OF YOUR INTERPRETATION

How do you know your perception of events is accurate? That your version of "reality" is one that both you and those around you can live with? Suppose you suffer not from bad things that happen, but from the way you *interpret* them?

This was the question posed by the pioneers of cognitive therapy—people like Albert Ellis and William Glasser. Their insight: a substantial difference exists between our experience and our interpretation of it.

Most of us operate on the assumption that reality is simply a series of events, some good and some bad. But of course, even as we're experiencing these events, we're also determining what they mean in terms of our own success and failure, happiness and unhappiness. Instead of R = E (Reality = Event), we actually live in a world where R = E + I (Reality = Event + Interpretation).

Who's doing the interpretation? We are, of course. And we're doing it all the time, in the privacy of our own brains. It's as though we're watching a sports event narrated by a play-by-play man and a color commentator.

Bored with the reality of play-by-play, we constantly add our own color commentary, without realizing the extent to which we are shaping and distorting reality.

Here's an example. Suppose a young man is interested in a young woman who works in the same office. Summoning his nerve, he goes over one day and asks her out. She thanks him but declines, saying that she is involved in a relationship with someone. He smiles and takes his leave.

That night, he's sitting at home thinking about the meaning of it all.

INSIDE HIS HEAD: Well, she turned me down. So what? It happens. People get turned down all the time. It's not just me . . . although I wonder why she wouldn't go out with me? I don't really believe that line about being involved with someone else. I think women just use that to let you down easy . . . I remember that girl Alison I asked out in high school, she told me she was dating a guy and I found out later it was a lie. So this is probably just bullshit . . .

Dammit, why do women have to lie? Why can't they just come out and say they're not attracted to you? At least, that would be honest. You'd know where you stand. But no, they have to beat around the bush and make up stories and then they wonder why men go crazy . . . It makes me so mad . . . I think I'm going to swear off women forever.

Notice that he shifts from the play-by-play—the simple recitation of the event—into the more fascinating world of color commentary. And that's where he gets in trouble. He transforms simple disappointment at being rejected into a general resentment toward womankind. Later on that evening, he'll probably begin to question his own attractiveness, making additional dents in what's left of his self-esteem. Given enough time, he may create a minor depression—despite the fact that his experience was essentially a routine one.

It's easy to see how the initial variable of emotional augmentation could escalate this into a relapse. Thus lesson two: as far as possible, skip the color commentary. When you start to interpret the meaning of a given experience, visualize a stop sign. Come to a complete halt. Ask yourself: What am I going to accomplish here? Am I increasing my understanding with all this thinking? Or am I just going over and over the same barren ground, beating the same already-dead horse, without changing anything?

3. IF YOU DON'T LIKE YOUR INTERPRETATION, TRY A DIFFERENT ONE

There's no law that says you must interpret events in one particular way. When you break off with a lover, you aren't *required* to interpret that as a sign you suffer from a hidden character flaw that makes you a failure in relationships. When your boss denies you a raise, you don't have to assume it's due to your own incompetence.

Nevertheless, many of us jump directly from the experience to such negative conclusions. Instead of wearing rose-colored glasses, ours are tinted black.

The way out is to remember that event and interpretation are inherently separate, just as there's a gap between what happens on the football field and what shows up in the sports pages the following morning. You can learn to silence your own color commentary before it talks you into a major depression.

For some of us, it's a struggle to believe that life is not really as awful as it seems. Our existence isn't that much worse than anyone else's—in fact, it's probably *better* than most. We experience more negative emotion, because of our tendency to interpret events in a negative fashion. But that we can change.

Start by examining your basic assumptions. Most of us believe that we simply respond to events as they occur. If something bad happens, we "have to" feel bad. Conversely, we assume that in order to feel good, things "have to" go our way.

Just as "reality" is a combination of external events and internal interpretation, so too is our response. It's that intermediate step—where we filter the event through our own information-processing systems—that permits us to alter our behavior. We can't change what happened. We can change the way we respond to it.

To do so, however, we have to overcome three obstacles:

1. *We tend to jump to conclusions.* This is understandable enough, because the human brain is designed to take tiny amounts of data and fill in the blanks. If only a small portion of an experience reminds us of a previous occurrence, we're prone to making unnecessary connections that aggravate our emotions.

2. *We tend to see ourselves as the center of a vast drama.* When we're kids, most of us view our lives as a movie in which we're the star and everyone else is a kind of bit player. As adults, we supposedly learn to see issues from other perspectives. Except when our emotions run high, in which case we leap right back on center stage.

3. *We have a terrific need to be right.* Part of the reason we have so many defense mechanisms is because we like to be "right" whenever possible. Life, on the other hand, is conspiring to make us "wrong." The solution, for most of us, is to *deny, rationalize, externalize,* or *minimize* our own errors. Our interpretation of events becomes a kind of wall between us and

reality—it's there not to explain events but to protect us from the unpleasant feeling of being wrong.

How to overcome these? Try the exercise below.

An Exercise

Step One

Take a given problem—say, a longstanding resentment that makes you mad whenever you think about it. Divide a sheet of paper into two columns. Write your resentment at the very top. Then at the beginning of the left-hand column, write: *What happened*. At the beginning of the right-hand column, write: *How I interpret it*. Go through the whole sequence of events, one by one, noting what transpired and your interpretation of it. For an example, see the following box:

WHAT HAPPENED	HOW I INTERPRET IT
Jack told me I was late with assignments.	He doesn't like me.
Marianne told me Jack was having problems at home.	He's taking his frustrations out on me.
My supervisor is leaving in three months and I haven't been told I have her job.	I'm not getting the promotion, probably because of Jack's prejudice against me. I'll never get anywhere here.

Step Two

Now take a second sheet of paper. Place it over the first sheet so that it covers the right-hand column, blocking out the list of your interpretations and leaving only the *What happened* column in view. At the top of the left side of the second page, write *Reinterpretation*. Take each occurrence, one by one, and come up with an alternate interpretation of its meaning. Make sure that it changes the outcome; in other words, that it makes it difficult for you to maintain your resentment. See the box below for an example. Of course, it won't seem natural. Do it anyway.

WHAT HAPPENED	REINTERPRETATION
Jack told me I was late with assignments.	I was late twice last month. Better watch it.
Marianne told me Jack was having problems at home.	He's probably a little preoccupied with his own troubles.
My supervisor is leaving in three months and I haven't been told I have her job.	They probably haven't decided yet. I should ask, however—let them know I want the job. And stay out of Jack's way.

Step Three

When done, compare and contrast the two lists of interpretations. The first list is the one you've always assumed was true. Fold the first sheet in half, cut it into two pieces, and throw the truth away. Now substitute the reinterpretation for the missing half.

Step Four

Act as though the reinterpretation is the truth. Base your behavior (including your approach to other people) on this new interpretation. Don't worry about whether or not your reinterpretation is accurate. Just act as if it is. See what happens.

THE PROBLEM
OF CRAVING

Craving is a normal desire that is temporarily intensified by deprivation. Dieters experience this: foods they might have ignored in the past seem unattainable delicacies. After a while, the craving loses some of its intensity, as the body adjusts to life without that particular substance.

Because sobriety involves depriving your brain and body of a drug it has come to expect, recovery from addiction always includes some degree of residual craving. Your body has convinced itself that it can't function without the drug, and doesn't understand why you're no longer providing it.

Naturally, craving is most intense at the beginning of recovery, when the body is struggling to adjust to its new, drug-free reality. Craving can persist in a less severe form (as any ex-smoker can attest) for months or years after the last exposure to the drug.

Early-stage craving is the most intense form, and is strongly related to extended withdrawal: it is rooted in changing bio-chemistry. *Mid-stage craving* makes its appearance a few months into sobriety, waxes and wanes in intensity, and usually accompanies fluctuations in mood. *Late-stage craving* is relatively mild and usually pops up during some activity associated with previous drug use: seeing an old drinking buddy, for example. When people say that craving lasts for years, it's this last type they refer to.

Most clinicians also separate low-level from high-level cravings. Examples of low-level cravings would include *vivid dreams,* usually a powerfully realistic vision of using the drug; *intrusive thoughts,* which pop in and out of your head during the course of the day; and *euphoric recall* of the good times associated with intoxication, similar in tone and content to the vivid dream.

High-level cravings include *selective memory,* which means that you find yourself unable to remember with any vividness the negative aspects of your addiction (this strongly reinforces euphoric memories and further distorts your view of reality); *planning* to get the drug (e.g., "If she's gone all weekend, I could get hold of a little bit of cocaine and have myself a party, and she'd never know."); and *acute drug hunger,* where the craving for the drug reaches a level of intensity reminiscent of what you may have experienced during acute withdrawal.

THERE ARE THREE RULES FOR DEALING WITH CRAVING

1. Remember that craving is natural. It isn't a sign of underlying psychological problems, weakness of will, or inevitable relapse. It's a normal part of the body's adjustment to life without a drug.

2. Learn techniques for reducing craving. Some are obvious: talking it over with an AA sponsor, getting vigorous exercise, removing yourself from a situation that reminds you of drug use. Remember: craving goes away by itself, usually in less than half an hour. If all else fails, just do something to take your mind off it while you wait for it to disappear. We've also included a visualization exercise below which you might find helpful.

3. *Don't dwell on craving.* Once it's abated, go back to doing something else. Over time, cravings become less intense, briefer in duration, and further apart.

A VISUALIZATION EXERCISE: BRAIN TELEVISION

This exercise is designed to help you control your cravings, especially the intrusive cravings that mark early recovery. The basic principle is simple: you learn to reduce the intensity of the craving sensation by associating it with the mental image of a colored sphere and then manipulating that image.

Start by picturing a television screen. Below it are three control knobs. The one on the left changes the channel. The one on the right controls the brightness of the picture. The one in the middle turns the set on and off.

Switch on the set. Reach out and turn the left knob one channel to the right. Gradually, something begins to appear on the screen: a dark blue sphere, very quiet and calming to look at. Observe it for a few seconds. Imagine that if you could reach out and touch it, it would feel pleasantly cool.

Reach out with your right hand and begin to turn the brightness dial to the right. Watch the sphere. As the knob turns, the sphere begins to change color: first a brighter blue, then gradually taking on a green tinge. Let the color shift more and more toward green, until the sphere is completely green. Stop turning the knob and observe the sphere for a few seconds. Note that the green color is very neutral; there is no particular feeling or sensation associated with it. If you were to touch it, it would feel neither hot nor cold.

Now, begin turning the knob to the right. As you do, you notice the sphere continues to change color, the green growing brighter and paler and then becoming tinged with red. The red sector gradually begins to dominate the sphere, and as it does, the sphere appears warmer, more intense. When the ball is completely red, stop and observe for a few seconds. If you were to touch it, you imagine, there would be a sensation of heat.

Then reach out and turn the brightness dial to the left. The green coloring begins to reappear. Gradually, the ball will become entirely green.

When it is completely green, stop for a second. Then resume turning the brightness knob toward the left. As you do, the sphere will change colors, once again shifting from green toward blue. As it does, your feelings will change: you will begin to feel relaxed, comfortable, in no particular hurry. You experience a pleasant sensation of coolness. When the sphere is dark blue, you will find you experience no craving at all. Instead you feel relaxed and refreshed.

Practice this several times, until you can clearly visualize the change in colors that accompanies turning the knob in either direction. When craving makes an appearance in the future, simply sit back for a moment, turn on the television set, look at the sphere, and begin turning the dial toward the blue range until you feel cool, relaxed, and composed.

An alternate suggestion:

Sometimes, the simplest way to rid yourself of intruding thoughts is simply to visualize your brain television, put the intrusive image on the screen, watch it for a few seconds, and then reach out and change the channel. Visualize something more pleasant—a beach scene, for example—and then switch the set off so you can return to what you were doing.

ASSESSING
YOUR
ATTITUDES

When it comes to addiction, there's no such thing as a "blank slate." We carry with us attitudes and beliefs that help shape our understanding of alcohol and drug problems.

Some of our opinions can be traced to childhood. Others are rooted in adult experience. We're even influenced (though we may bitterly deny it) by half-digested episodes of *Oprah*. This potpourri of information becomes the lens through which we view what we call reality.

When we learn something that contradicts our existing beliefs, we experience a sort of "cognitive dissonance"—a disagreeable sensation that what we're hearing *can't* be true. To overcome this, we must distance ourselves from this initial response and gain some perspective. Otherwise, we remain blind to the causes of relapse, even when they're right in front of us. We can't "see" them, because we're looking for something else.

Thus we begin our discussion of relapse prevention by taking a look at the attitudes we bring with us. We unearth these beliefs with a simple self-test.

_____ WHAT'S YOUR RELAPSE MODEL? _____

Read over the following questions, and rate your response to each on a scale of 1 to 4, with each number representing the following:

1. strongly disagree
2. somewhat disagree
3. somewhat agree
4. strongly agree

Then total your score for each of the eight categories in the blank provided following the category. Instructions for determining and understanding your score are at the end of the questionnaire.

Group A

1. I sometimes suspect that treatment is a waste of time—that no matter what, the great majority of alcoholics and addicts return to drinking or drugs.

    Rating: _____

2. I believe some people possess a basic flaw that makes it impossible for them to live without alcohol or drugs.

    Rating: _____

3. Even when I know someone is sober, I sometimes suspect they're still drinking secretly—or that sooner or later they'll go back to alcohol or drugs.

    Rating: _____

4. I think a lot of these people who claim to be recovering addicts and alcoholics were never really alcoholic in the first place.

Rating: _____

5. Probably 90% of alcoholics and addicts return to drugs at one point or another.

Rating: _____

Total: _____

Group B

6. I believe that recovery depends on having a personal experience of spiritual conversion and dedication to God.

Rating: _____

7. I feel that religion and church attendance are the only real way to recover from alcohol and drug problems.

Rating: _____

8. I think alcoholics and addicts need someone to keep an eye on them and to make sure they don't stray from the flock.

Rating: _____

9. I believe that many people would stay away from drugs and alcohol if they had someone who really loved them.

Rating: _____

10. It's important to remove all sources of temptation—otherwise the addict won't be able to resist it.

Rating: _____

Total: _____

Group C

11. I think staying sober is largely a matter of individual willpower.

Rating: _____

12. The main reason for relapse is lack of motivation.

Rating: 1

13. Relapse is a sign of immaturity.

Rating: 1

14. Alcoholics are people who don't exercise good judgment in drinking situations.

Rating: 4

15. I think alcohol and drugs are just an easy way to avoid taking responsibility for your problems.

Rating: 3

Total: 12

Group D

16. The best way to keep an alcoholic sober is to let them know that they're killing themselves.

Rating: 1

17. I think alcohol and drugs are just a way of committing slow suicide.

Rating: 1

18. Alcoholism and drug addiction are different from cancer and heart disease because they are self-induced.

Rating: 1

19. Alcoholics and addicts are people who don't care enough about their health.

Rating: 1

20. Physical withdrawal lasts a few days. After that, the addiction is largely psychological.

Rating: 1

Total: 8

Group E

21. People relapse because they haven't accepted their powerlessness over alcohol and drugs.

    Rating: ____

22. A lot of people relapse because they haven't really hit
bottom yet.

    Rating: ____

23. To prevent relapse, attend more AA meetings and work the
Steps.

    Rating: ____

24. Relapse occurs because alcohol and drugs are cunning,
baffling, and powerful.

    Rating: ____

25. A relapser is someone who hasn't gotten really honest with
himself.

    Rating: ____
    Total: ____

Group F

26. People relapse because they haven't worked through their
underlying emotional problems.

    Rating: ____

27. Alcoholics relapse because of their low self-esteem.

    Rating: ____

28. People who give up alcohol and drugs without dealing with
their psychological problems will just turn to food, gambling, or some other addiction.

    Rating: ____

29. Some people just have an addictive personality. They'll
always be addicted to something.

    Rating: ____

30. The great majority of addicts and alcoholics drink and use drugs in order to self-medicate a psychiatric problem.

Rating: _____ 3

Total: _____ /8

Group G

31. People relapse because they aren't able to cope with reality.

Rating: _____ 3

32. Addicts and alcoholics relapse because they can't handle stress.

Rating: _____ 3

33. Drinking and drug use are simple bad habits. Relapse occurs because habits are hard to break.

Rating: _____ 3

34. I believe that some alcoholics can learn to control their drinking through behavior modification.

Rating: _____ 1

35. Addicts and alcoholics need to find alternate sources of gratification to substitute for alcohol and drugs.

Rating: _____ 3

Total: _____ /3

Group H

36. Many people return to alcohol and drugs because they were raised in a dysfunctional family.

Rating: _____ 1

37. Most people relapse because of untreated co-dependency.

Rating: _____ 1

38. Unless the whole family is willing to change, relapse is unavoidable.

Rating: _____ 1

39. I believe the only effective treatment for addiction is intensive family therapy.

   Rating: _____

40. Alcoholics and addicts relapse because they have unresolved issues regarding intimacy, trust, and shame.

   Rating: _____
   Total: _____

Finished? Add up the totals in each group of five questions. Rank the eight categories from highest to lowest score. The higher the score, the more that particular model has influenced your approach to addiction and its treatment. Your strongest models are those with the three highest scores.

Now: Read the following section to determine how those three models influence the way you will respond to the demands of treatment and the possibility of relapse.

GROUP A:
_____ THE IMPAIRED MODEL _____

You naturally assume that recovery is difficult, if not impossible. For you, the issue of treatment and relapse is surrounded by an aura of futility. You may suspect that people in AA and NA still drink or use drugs from time to time and are simply concealing it from the outside world. You reject the idea that most addicts can learn to live without alcohol and drugs. In your eyes, being alcoholic or addicted is similar to having the most severe form of cancer—despite brief periods of remission, the ultimate outcome is predetermined.

Obviously, this is the worst sort of approach with which to begin recovery. Try to think where you got it. What experiences shaped your thinking? Was it personal contact with an alcoholic or addict who continued to drink, didn't respond to intervention, and perhaps died of the disease? Was it through stories told by members of your family, or "legends" concerning relatives or family friends? Opinions formed through interaction with your peers? Something you learned in school? Articles you read that made treatment seem hopeless?

People who hold such beliefs and yet find themselves in a treatment program often hide these attitudes from those around them. They fear being branded as "unmotivated" or being a negative influence on others who are trying to recover. Don't make that mistake. If you find yourself thinking that no matter what steps you take, relapse (and perhaps eventual death from addictive disease) is *inevitable,* discuss it with a counselor, Twelve Step sponsor, or others in a group. This belief system— like all the others we describe—is learned. Therefore, it can also be *unlearned.*

TENETS OF THE IMPAIRED MODEL

Definition of Addiction: Chronic excessive drinking or drug use.

Source of Model: Popular myth that alcoholics never recover; experience with chronic relapsers.

Cause of Addiction: Unknown; alcoholics and addicts are "just that way."

Treatment: None. Nothing can change the addict. The most you can do is to provide custodial care.

Cause of Relapse: Inevitable result of innate flaw.

Potential Problems in Recovery: A sense of hopelessness. Subconsciously, you'll assume that whatever you do won't be enough—that you're doomed to ultimate failure.

How to Change: Do Exercise A on page 277.

GROUP B:
THE DRY MORAL MODEL

You tend to view alcoholism and drug dependency as primarily a *moral* and *spiritual* problem, which is best addressed by and through the church. You see alcohol and drugs as inherently evil, and feel that addiction is in some respects a punishment for sinfulness. To your way of thinking, people who drink or use drugs stray from God and the path of righteousness, and pay the price. Ultimately, they have no one to blame but themselves. You do, however, believe in redemption, perhaps through repentance.

Because you blame addiction on alcohol and drugs, you believe strongly in total abstinence. You see recovery as a return to the fold, and the mechanism for recovery may be what is known as a *conversion experience.* The alcoholic or addict, recoiling at his own fall from grace, reaches out to God and is healed. The desire to drink or use drugs is removed, the soul is cleansed, the past is forgiven. From that moment, the addict devotes his life to the service of God and his fellow man, and testifies as to his transformation so that others might be inspired.

You will assume that relapse is brought about by the temptations of alcohol and drugs coupled with a temporary lapse in faith. In fact, you may see recovery as a covenant with God and relapse as a breach of that covenant—a very heavy burden for any human being to bear, as the Bible repeatedly makes plain.

Such beliefs come from your family and your early religious training. Although the dry moral model has no scientific basis, it does contribute to recovery simply because of its insistence on complete abstinence. But the downside is that it requires an unquestioning belief in certain dogma that many people simply cannot accept—which was one of the reasons for the growth of the spiritual alternative of Twelve Step fellowships.

TENETS OF THE DRY MORAL MODEL

Definition of Addiction: Excessive drinking or drug use.

Source of Model: Organized religion, especially Protestant, Muslim, and evangelical churches.

Cause of Addiction: Moral turpitude and estrangement from God.

Treatment: Abstinence, rigorous church attendance.

Cause of Relapse: Insufficient faith in God; succumbing to temptation.

Potential Problems in Recovery: A tendency toward excessive guilt and self-castigation. This model depends on a spiritual "conversion experience" and if it does not occur, you may feel you are somehow less than your fellows. You may be very hard on yourself and assume that only through self-hate can you achieve redemption.

How to Change: Do Exercise B on pages 277–78.

GROUP C:
_____ THE WET MORAL MODEL _____

Congratulations—your view is in line with that of the majority of Americans. You believe that addiction is a sign of immaturity, irresponsibility, and weakness of will. Thus you tend to think of alcoholism and drug dependency as alcohol and drug *abuse*—the implication being that the addict is abusing the substance and therefore at fault for whatever happens as a result.

Treatment, in your view, is the assumption of responsibility. It includes both moral education and a commitment to "do the right thing." In fact, given improvement in these areas, you probably suspect that the alcoholic should be able to drink "responsibly." This, after all, is the model that gave birth to *controlled drinking* programs where alcoholics strove to regain control of their consumption under the watchful eye of the scientific community.

Because a return to drugs is seen as technically possible (even desirable), you probably think of relapse as *overdrinking* or *overusing.* You also carry a hidden agenda into the treatment process—you believe that eventually you will regain control over alcohol or drugs. Sure, you'll abstain for a while. But sooner or later, you'll want to engage in a little experiment to see if perhaps you have, as a result of your new knowledge and commitment, restored your ability to drink or use drugs in a controlled fashion. You'll balk at the first of the Twelve Steps, because of the implications of powerlessness and un-manageability. You're most likely quite angry or frustrated at your own loss of control, and embarrassed and ashamed of what you regard as your "weakness." You are afraid others will mistake you for "one of those people." Because you demonstrate consider-able self-control in other areas, you are baffled by your failure in this respect. For you, alcoholism is an accusation rather than a diagnosis, and you regard it as a matter of personal pride to avoid it at all costs. You see abstinence not as a solution but as an admission of defeat.

TENETS OF THE WET MORAL MODEL

Definition of Addiction: Loss of control over alcohol or drug use.

Source of Model: Experience of non-alcoholic drinkers.

Cause of Addiction: Personal weakness; underdeveloped sense of right and wrong.

Treatment: Increased willpower; punishment for episodes of loss of control.

Cause of Relapse: Inadequate self-discipline or disregard for mo-rality.

Potential Problems in Recovery: A "war within" yourself. Rather than accept abstinence, you'll battle to regain control over alcohol or drugs. Regarding yourself as weak-willed, you'll be ashamed and reluctant to seek help from others. You see recovery as a failure.

How to Change: Do Exercise C on page 278.

GROUP D:
THE OLD MEDICAL MODEL

You view the alcoholic as the "perpetrator" rather than the victim of addiction. You feel that if you hadn't used alcohol or drugs excessively, you would not have become alcoholic. Conversely, you feel that once free of the physical addiction, you should be able to control your impulses through an exercise of will. You feel that the best motivation for sobriety is the knowledge that death or illness awaits the relapser. Health is very important to you, and even when addicted you worry about possible consequences and try to maintain a diet and exercise regimen. You'll view recovery as an opportunity to reach new heights of good health.

The downside is that you may overreact to any medical problems that you cannot control. People who give up alcohol and drugs frequently have various chronic aches, pains, and allergies, or have difficulty sleeping. It's harmless, but your preoccupation with "feeling good" may contribute to unrealistic expectations.

TENETS OF THE OLD MEDICAL MODEL

Definition of Addiction: Chronic excessive drinking or drug use.
Source of Model: Medical profession.

Cause of Addiction: Physical withdrawal and organ damage brought about by excess drinking or drug use; addiction is "self-induced" disease.

Treatment: Medical detoxification and fear of health consequences if drinking or drug use continues.

Cause of Relapse: Poor attention to health; innate self-destructive tendencies.

Potential Problems in Recovery: Ignoring long-term aspects of recovery. You may assume that once physical problems have passed, you can return to alcohol or drugs safely.

How to Change: Do Exercise D on page 278.

GROUP E:
THE ALCOHOLICS ANONYMOUS (AA) MODEL

You've obviously had some exposure to AA and its offshoots—Narcotics Anonymous, Cocaine Anonymous, Al-Anon, and the like. You believe that recovery is largely a matter of abstinence, attending meetings, and working the Twelve Steps. You have faith that anyone who sticks with AA will ultimately meet with success. You're probably aware that many of the first hundred members of AA were chronic relapsers before entering the fellowship.

Like most in AA, you tend to regard short relapses as "slips" which are much less serious than extended binges. You may believe that the principal cause of relapse is a lack of "rigorous honesty" in your practice of the program. You may also emphasize the importance of dealing with character defects in maintaining sobriety.

TENETS OF THE ALCOHOLICS ANONYMOUS MODEL

Definition of Addiction: Chronic excessive drinking or drug use.

Source of Model: AA and similar Twelve Step fellowships.

Cause of Addiction: A combination of physical allergy and mental obsession.

Treatment: Abstinence and Twelve Step meeting attendance.

Cause of Relapse: Lack of personal honesty; insufficient involvement in Twelve Step group.

Potential Problems in Recovery: Though AA and related groups are the most valuable tools that recovering people have, they do not have a systematic approach to relapse. Many relapsers drop out of these groups before they have a chance to experience their benefits, and do not return.

How to Change: Do Exercise E on pages 278–79.

GROUP F:
_____ THE PSYCHODYNAMIC MODEL _____

You're a devotee of psychology and, when confronted with a problem, naturally look for a psychological explanation. You tend to focus on underlying emotional issues rather than on specific behavior. You find it easy to believe in an "addictive personality," of which alcohol and drug use is merely a symptom. If alcoholic yourself, you worry about what you'll be like when alcohol and drugs are no longer available to "mask" your feelings. You suspect that sobriety is only a half-measure—that you won't truly be "well" until you've analyzed the root causes of your drinking or drug use, through psychotherapy and self-examination.

On a less obvious level, you may wonder if you couldn't return to occasional drinking or use of certain "mild" drugs after a period of abstinence and intensive therapy. You suspect you may need such chemical assistance to "cope" with your inner turmoil. The upside of your approach is your willingness to examine your own motives. The downside is your preoccupation with self-analysis instead of productive action.

TENETS OF THE PSYCHODYNAMIC MODEL

Definition of Addiction: Excessive or inappropriate use of alcohol or drugs.

Source of Model: Psychological and psychoanalytic theory.

Cause of Addiction: Underlying personality disorder.

Treatment: Long-term psychotherapy aimed at insight into childhood antecedents of addictive personality.

Cause of Relapse: Avoidance of painful feelings through return to drinking or drugs; "self-medication" of psychiatric problems.

Potential Problems in Recovery: Getting lost in the past. You may seek to change the present by changing the way you feel about events of long ago. This is an extremely time consuming and expensive process that frequently fails to achieve the desired result. You may also "de-value" sobriety.

How to Change: Do Exercise F on page 279.

GROUP G:
THE BEHAVIORIST MODEL

You believe that alcoholism and drug dependency are at root bad habits—a series of learned or conditioned responses. Like someone in the wet moral model, you take the position that the point of treatment is to restore your control over your own impulses. You're attracted to behavior-modification programs and their promise of reconditioning.

The central theme of your approach is always *self-control*. This probably applies to more than alcoholism; it's a central precept of your philosophy of life. You are mistrustful of anything that appears to remove responsibility from the individual—including the idea that alcoholism is a disease. You suspect that this idea "encourages" irresponsibility and antisocial behavior. You may find yourself philosophically bound to the idea that given proper conditioning and personal commitment, one can learn to drink or use certain "recreational" drugs in a controlled fashion.

You feel that an important part of this is to confine your drinking or drug use to the "right" situations, and to avoid using alcohol or drugs for the "wrong" reasons. The upside is that you're more than willing to make significant changes in your behavior, even those requiring considerable sacrifice. The downside is that you're another ripe candidate for the "war within": that endless, futile struggle to regain control over your own body's response to a chemical.

TENETS OF THE BEHAVIORIST MODEL

Definition of Addiction: Excessive or inappropriate use of alcohol or drugs.

Source of Model: Behavioral psychology.

Cause of Addiction: Learned behavior gives birth to self-destructive habit pattern.

Treatment: Behavior modification through reward and punishment.

Cause of Relapse: Environmental triggers produce return to old habits and negative coping mechanisms.

Potential Problems in Recovery: Overemphasis on behavioral instead of attitudinal change. May attempt to return to controlled drinking or drug use as test of your new "coping skills."

How to Change: Do Exercise G on page 279.

GROUP H:
_____ THE FAMILY SYSTEMS MODEL _____

You view most things in terms of relationships between people, especially those within a family. You are very psychologically oriented, though you tend to emphasize family dynamics rather than personality. You believe in an "addictive family" which shapes the lives of its members and points them toward addiction or co-dependency. These patterns begin in childhood—the "family of origin"—and are repeated in adult relationships. You are as interested in the affected family member as you are in the alcoholic or addict, and you believe that treatment can't be successful unless it includes the entire family.

You suspect that relapse is largely a product of unresolved issues within the family. You are mistrustful of sobriety that doesn't include extensive examination of family background and relationships—of someone who gets "dry" but doesn't come to terms with their origins. In this you have much in common with those in the psychodynamic model. The upside of your approach is your acute awareness of the complex patterns of enabling that develop within the family afflicted by addiction. The downside is that you may de-emphasize the person with the disease. Your model is probably better for treating the co-dependent than for treating the addict.

TENETS OF THE FAMILY SYSTEMS MODEL

Definition of Addiction: Drinking or drug use that adversely affects relationships with others, especially within the family.

Source of Model: Family therapists.

Cause of Addiction: Pathological or dysfunctional family system.

Treatment: Family therapy.

Cause of Relapse: Unresolved issues within the family.

Potential Problems in Recovery: Overemphasis on the behavior of others. You may believe your recovery depends on the cooperation of those around you; if they are uncooperative, you may regard that as excuse to relapse.

How to Change: Do Exercise H on page 279.

Remember: each model has its strengths and weaknesses. But to prevent relapse, we must set aside some of our attitudes and beliefs in favor of new ones—in particular what we call the chronic disease model, which holds that addiction is a chronic, progressive, primary, and potentially fatal disease. Left untreated, this disease will probably kill you many years before your time. With proper treatment, it is eminently survivable. That's the trick: giving your disease the proper treatment. Once again, that's what this book is about.

Now, having examined both the disease and our attitudes toward it, we're ready for a close look at the twelve traps that lead to relapse—with suggestions for avoiding them.

PART TWO: THE TWELVE TRAPS OF RELAPSE

TREATMENT
FAILURES

The first three traps reflect a failure of the treatment process. We should begin by reviewing the difference between a *cure* and a *treatment*. Most people use them interchangeably, and that's incorrect.

In medicine, we achieve a cure when we are able to rid the patient of the various signs and symptoms of a disease and return him or her to the premorbid (predisease) state. A cure for alcoholism, for example, would mean the alcoholic could once again use the drug for social or recreational purposes without fear of dependence or loss of control. Despite the claims of some behavioral scientists, we have no reliable evidence that this occurs. In fact, we have considerable experience indicating that it doesn't. Thus alcoholism is currently classified as an *incurable* disease. And because the organ primarily involved in addiction—the brain—is so complex, there's a chance a cure may never exist.

A treatment, on the other hand, is a medical or behavioral intervention that reduces the signs and symptoms that accompany a disease. Insulin supplements, for example, are a treatment for diabetes, but they do not represent a cure. Antihypertensive medications reduce the risk of heart attack, but they do not restore the heart to its premorbid state.

The primary treatment for addictive disease is *abstinence* from addictive drugs. The abstinent alcoholic is relieved of the various symptoms of alcoholism—including those that are potentially fatal. But the physiological adaptations that support the disease remain intact. We have done nothing to eradicate them. Should the alcoholic choose to reintroduce the drug, he risks the return of painful symptoms. Treatment, therefore, is the *process by which you establish and maintain stable abstinence.*

This is accomplished through the completion of four simple but sometimes difficult tasks:

1. You learn about the disease. Most of us enter treatment in a state of profound ignorance about the illness that afflicts us. We probably can't define it; we may not even realize we have a disease. Thus our first task is know our enemy: to learn how we came to be in a treatment program, despite our best efforts to avoid it.

2. You self-diagnose. Once we have a body of knowledge about addiction, we need to apply that learning by identifying the signs and symptoms of the disease in our own experience. The reason is obvious: unless we come to the conclusion that we suffer from a chronic disease, we can't be expected to *treat* it on a continuing basis. This is why the phrase "I am an alcoholic (or addict)" is repeated so often at AA meetings. It's the motivation for recovery.

3. You become involved in recovery groups. Most people recover through their involvement in Alcoholics Anonymous or similar fellowships. These groups offer support and guidance essential to recovery, and carry the added benefit of being both free and widely available.

4. *You assume personal responsibility for your own recovery.* When we enter treatment, we're usually *externalizing* the causes of our drug use onto outside forces: family problems, job stress, childhood trauma. In treatment, we learn that the responsibility for success or failure rests solely with us. No matter who we are or where we come from, we bear the burden of recovery equally. No one—no matter how gifted or well-intentioned— can do it for us.

If you don't accomplish these tasks, it's only a matter of time until you relapse. You needn't do anything else "wrong." In fact, if you fail to meet these four challenges, you'll probably resume drinking or drug use during or shortly after completing the treatment program.

Thus the first three relapse traps we'll discuss in this chapter have to do with common mistakes made in attempting to complete these four tasks.

THE FIRST TRAP: NOT FOLLOWING DIRECTIONS

"At some of these [steps] we balked. We thought we could find an easier, softer way. But we could not. With all the earnestness at our command, we beg of you to be fearless and thorough from the very start."

—Alcoholics Anonymous,
The Big Book, Chapter 5,
"How It Works"

Most of us conceive of change as internally motivated. We assume that an alteration in our feelings leads us to revise our thinking and subsequently our actions. This might be diagrammed as follows:

Altered Feelings = Altered Thinking = Altered Behavior

But recovery from addiction follows a very different pattern. In fact, it's the *reverse*.

Altered Behavior = Altered Thinking = Altered Feelings

Change begins with action. After a while, we become intellectually and emotionally comfortable with our new behavior.

Here's an illustration of the difference between change as it occurs in conventional therapy and as it happens in addictions treatment. First, a therapy patient:

Becky's Story

Becky experienced longstanding problems in relationships with men. No matter how she tried to please them, they always seemed to grow dissatisfied and eventually leave her. After one such breakup, she became depressed and at the urging of her friends entered therapy. Encouraged to explore her experience in an open-ended way, she identified an underlying feeling of personal worthlessness. She came to understand that she resented ignoring her own needs to satisfy others, and that she communicated this resentment to those she was involved with—thus driving them away. Motivated by her insight, she took steps to increase her self-esteem by altering the thinking patterns that reinforced it. Gradually, she allowed herself to risk another relationship, and was gratified to discover that she was able to maintain the involvement in a healthier fashion.

Now, an alcoholic as he initiates treatment:

Vernon's Story

Vernon saw a therapist briefly after his divorce. Talking about his marital problems made his depression worse, so he dropped out. Admittedly, he was drinking a lot, but he felt this was justified by the emotional trauma of losing his family. As soon as the settlement was final and he began to feel better, he would cut back. But for now, he needed all the help he could get.

During this period, Vernon was arrested twice for drunk driving. The judge suspended his license and referred him into a counseling program. Vernon felt this was entirely unwarranted and suspected it was due to political pressure from Mothers Against Drunk Driving.

At the court's direction, Vernon began to attend meetings of AA. He hated AA because of the long, boring stories and the fact that he was forced to associate with common alcoholics. Though his probation forbade it, he drank secretly until caught by his probation officer and warned that it could result in the permanent revocation of his license. Motivated by fear, Vernon swore off alcohol. He told himself it was only temporary. But to his surprise, life began to improve. After a few days, his depression seemed to lessen. At first, it was very uncomfortable being around his old friends, but he found he made other friends among the people at AA, who weren't really so bad once you got to know them. Vernon started to look forward to the meetings. A year later, the restrictions were removed from his license. And he found he didn't *want* to celebrate with alcohol.

Becky begins to improve as she gains insight into her emotions. Vernon, on the other hand, gains no insight until he quits drinking. The reason: their problems are different. Becky's is one of self-esteem. Vernon suffers from a progressive disease. For the addict, *action often precedes understanding.*

As a result of his decision to abstain, Vernon experiences a number of unanticipated rewards. These reinforce the value of abstinence and help him to develop insight into the source of his earlier difficulties. Had he not been forced to give up drinking, he may never have achieved that level of self-knowledge.

Where insight is limited and denial is the rule, following directions becomes all important. Newly recovering addicts are asked to adhere to a set of instructions that generally include the following:

1. Abstain from alcohol and other drugs.
2. Attend meetings of Twelve Step groups.
3. Make changes in your daily routine to reinforce sobriety.
4. Change your associations to reduce risk of relapse.

These instructions may come from physicians, psychiatrists, counselors, therapists, sponsors, or knowledgeable peers. Anyone who has trouble seeking out or taking advice from others is in for a rough ride. Some of us are just a lot better than others at making changes in the way we live. Some of us just *hate* having to do things differently.

ATTITUDE CHECK #1: FOLLOWING DIRECTIONS

To find out how well you take direction from others, answer yes or no to the following statements.

1. I've never felt comfortable taking directions from authority figures.
2. I am suspicious of the motives of people who give advice about personal problems.
3. As a rule, I don't like to rely on other people.
4. When traveling in a strange area, I find myself very reluctant to stop and ask for directions.
5. I think that when the chips are down, the only person you can trust is yourself.
6. Most people would characterize me as a stubborn person.
7. My first reaction to being told what to do is negative.

8. I believe no one knows how to solve my problems as well as I do.

9. I always look for a shortcut—an easier way to reach my goal.

10. I find I hate being told what to do, no matter what the circumstances.

11. I'd rather figure out how to do something on my own than seek advice from others.

12. I think it's always better if you're able to solve a problem on your own rather than asking for help.

13. I don't believe that doctors and counselors really know what's best or have my best interests in mind.

14. I've always been something of a rebel.

15. If I'm at a red light, and it's late at night and there isn't any traffic around, I feel perfectly justified in running that light. After all, who does it hurt?

Look at the box that follows for an interpretation of the results.

If you answered "yes" to one or two of the questions your chance of relapse is low. If you answered "yes" to three or four of the questions your chance of relapse is moderate and you should continue to learn and be aware of the pitfalls of recovery. If you answered "yes" to five or six of the questions you are at high risk for relapse and should pay particular attention to this trap. If you answered "yes" to seven or more of the questions you are in a relapse "red zone" and need to seek and follow good advice immediately.

If you're in the last two categories, you're going to have some difficulty treating a chronic disease such as alcoholism or drug dependency. You'll need to be aware of this and to make a conscious effort to change. Start with the exercises at the end of this chapter on p. 76.

WHAT IS THE SOURCE OF NONCOMPLIANCE?

Compliance is especially important because we don't possess a *cure* for addictive disease. When doctors can't cure an illness, they are forced to transfer the responsibility for treatment to the patient. The patient, unfortunately, has other things on his mind.

There are probably as many reasons for noncompliance as there are human beings, but here are a few important ones.

1. A desire for comfort and convenience

Most of us like things to be comfortable. Unfortunately, recovery involves change, and change always includes a degree of discomfort. The two goals are contradictory, and our search for convenience often undermines treatment. Here's an example.

Brian's Story

Brian's wife has insisted that he go to a treatment program if he wants to save his marriage. He objects that she is being unreasonable. "You're proposing that I drop everything," he says. "I'm not like these rich guys that can afford to check into Betty Ford for the weekend."

"What about that outpatient program we talked about?" she said.

"They want me to go every night for two weeks. There's no way I can do that. I don't work all day so I can spend my few hours of leisure time in some group-therapy session."

"Brian . . ."

"There you go again. I recognize that tone. Look, I know

I've done some things wrong, but that's no reason for you to try to have me locked up for a month, or ask me to sacrifice the only time of the day I have with my family, or condemn myself to sit in some AA meeting with drunks who just got out of jail. And besides, I've already quit drinking. It's been three and a half weeks. Three months if you don't count that one weekend. I think I've already shown I can do it on my own."

Note the catchwords in Brian's arguments: he demands that treatment be "reasonable" and "fair." Unfortunately, he's dealing with a disease that can be profoundly *un*reasonable and *un*fair.

The desire for comfort is often expressed in what is known as cutting corners: following some but not all of the directions of a recovery program. This, too, can render it ineffective. When relapse occurs, the addict is puzzled. "I don't understand it," he says to himself. "I did everything they told me to." In reality, he did *part* of what was advised.

2. Fear of treatment itself

Some people become noncompliant because they're more afraid of treatment than of the disease. The idea of acknowledging a drug or alcohol problem may seem like a ticket to public humiliation. Sometimes it threatens something important: a job, a relationship, standing in the community, self-respect. To some, the treatment center has a sign over the door that reads: "Abandon hope all ye who enter here."

This isn't much different from a woman with a lump on her breast who refuses to go to the doctor. In her mind, a "treatment" that may mean losing a breast is more worrisome than the possibility of cancer.

3. Minimizing the need for help

Everyone knows that alcoholics and addicts traditionally underestimate their level of involvement with alcohol or drugs. Thus the problem you seek to remedy may not be anywhere near as complex as the one you really have. The treatment you're willing to accept reflects this minimalist view of your illness. Here's an example:

Eddie's Story

Eddie, an art student, has always been a heavy user of marijuana. In the past two years, he's begun using LSD on a regular basis "as an aid to creativity." Eddie believes that drugs should be legalized for responsible users and that LSD is an integral part of the creative process necessary to bring forth his art. A few months ago, however, Eddie was arrested by the campus police for "streaking" naked through the Student Union while tripping. He does not recall the episode or the circumstances leading up to it. Though his parents want him to seek counseling, Eddie insists that he does not really have a drug problem, and that since he now knows better, he will be able to avoid further problems. "I learned my lesson," he insists.

HOW THE TRAP CLOSES

Once the fundamental error in thinking has been made, subsequent decisions and behavior follow a predictable pattern. It goes something like this:

The underlying assumption: You convince yourself that you are capable of treating addiction without outside guidance.

Resulting behavior: When given directions, you either fail to follow them or "cheat" by ignoring key aspects of recovery. You avoid formal treatment altogether or seek treatment that has little structure and makes minimal demands on your time and attention.

The second decision: If able to remain abstinent for a while, you interpret that as a sign that your underlying assumption was correct and that you can therefore further reduce your involvement in treatment.

Resulting behavior: You attempt to handle various difficulties without seeking outside help, as "tests" of your sobriety.

The third decision: Somewhere during this period you will have a "slip." When that happens, you will consider seeking additional help—but will probably reject that in favor of more reliance on "willpower." You'll justify that by pointing to your earlier successes.

Resulting behavior: You'll make excuses for each slip, blaming them on social problems, stress, or other people. You will become preoccupied with these problems rather than with the need to maintain abstinence.

The fourth decision: At some point, another crisis will occur, and you will once again consider seeking additional treatment. You will probably reject it in favor of "giving up" on yourself—deciding that treatment doesn't work in your case and that people like you probably "have" to drink or use drugs.

Resulting behavior: Continued drinking or drug use with mounting signs of loss of control. Often, this is punctuated by extended binges.

As you might imagine, periods of control or abstinence grow shorter while the periods of loss of control become longer and more numerous. Suggestions from others are met with fight-or-flight responses, or with meaningless promises to deal with the problem on your own. When you fail, you respond with increasing self-recrimination, depression, and frustration, along with vows to do better next time.

RED FLAGS

We laugh at people who talk to themselves, but the fact is, most of us talk to ourselves most of the time—we just don't do it aloud. This inner dialogue, or *self-talk*, if we pay attention to it, can reveal when we are entering each relapse trap. Look and listen for any of the following:

1. I know myself. I can do this my way.
2. I don't have the time to invest in treatment.
3. I'm not that bad yet. If I ever get that far, then I'll get help.
4. Who knows if treatment would work anyway? I've known people who did it according to the book and fell flat on their faces. And I've heard of people who did it on their own.
5. I've got other commitments. I can't just drop everything.
6. I caught it early. I'm not as bad as most.
7. I've always been the kind to stick to something once I've made up my mind.
8. Well, I've done most of the stuff they tell you to do. And I'm sober, aren't I? It's working.

If you find yourself thinking along these lines, you're skirting the edges of this relapse trap.

RELAPSE IN ACTION

The Story of Melvin Sanders

Melvin's wife, Betty, insisted that he seek help for his drinking. She initially wanted him to enter a hospital for a month. That was simply out of the question. It took three weeks of negotiations before he and Betty agreed on a compromise. Melvin would see a psychiatrist. Perhaps he could get to the root of his problems, and eliminate this insane compulsion to drink.

Melvin left the office after his initial session feeling encouraged by the way the doctor had validated Melvin's own feelings about how difficult it was to cope with today's world. But he was discouraged at the psychiatrist's insistence on giving Melvin medications. The first drug was apparently something to make him feel less depressed. The second was something that would make him sick if he drank alcohol.

"*Any* alcohol?" he had asked incredulously. "Even a beer?"

The medications became Melvin's particular stumbling block. He didn't like the way the antidepressant made him feel, so he decided not to take it. And the other drug seemed to Melvin to be downright dangerous. Suppose somebody slipped him a drink at a party as a joke? So Melvin decided to terminate the medications—he never actually took them after the first dose or two. Not wanting to offend the psychiatrist, he decided it would be his own little secret.

The psychiatrist had also made a point of instructing Melvin to attend meetings of Alcoholics Anonymous. Mel felt this was excessive. In the first place, Mel had a job, and he was under the impression most members of AA were chronically unemployed. Secondly, he wouldn't dream of exposing himself to the kind of public ridicule he would have to endure if the other car salesmen ever discovered he was no better than a common drunk. Good Lord, he might never work again.

Therapy progressed at what Melvin and the doctor seemed to agree was a satisfactory rate. As far as the psychiatrist knew, Melvin was using both medicines and attending AA meetings. Mel felt this small deception was justified because he had not in fact violated the *intent* of the medication—he was not inordinately depressed, and he was maintaining abstinence. In Mel's view, that was proof the medicine had been unnecessary in the first place. And since AA was not actually a medical organization, Melvin felt justified in not adhering to that particular part of the treatment regimen. "It's not like he asked me to see another professional," Melvin reasoned. "He just wants me to pour my heart out to a bunch of strangers. I don't see how that would help."

The other area where Mel had not been entirely truthful with the therapist was over the issue of abstinence from alcohol. When Melvin assured the therapist he was "not drinking," he meant that he was not drinking anywhere near as much or as often as he had been drinking before he got into therapy. When he said he was "totally abstinent," he meant he rigorously avoided the beverages that he believed led to most of his problems: vodka and other forms of hard spirits. He still had an occasional beer or a glass of wine with dinner, when he wasn't with Betty or one of the other people who wouldn't understand. In Melvin's eyes, he had blazed new trails in establishing and maintaining a kind of *virtual* abstinence which in his mind was far superior to the rigid, fanatical brand of abstinence practiced by AA.

Unfortunately, Melvin wasn't able to maintain his standard. He got drunk on Thanksgiving Day after a particularly horrendous dinner at the home of his hated sister-in-law. In the morning he called the psychiatrist and told him what happened.

"I think perhaps you ought to go into a treatment program, Mel," the doctor opined.

"Now, I don't think we ought to be that hasty here, Doc," Mel said. "There were a lot of different circumstances involved . . ."

"Your wife told me that you've been drinking the entire time you've been seeing me."

"*What?* That's a lie." Mel was thinking, *How the hell did she know that?* "I think you're overreacting. Maybe I haven't been that good about the alcohol. But you said I had a living problem." Mel, feeling his last support crumbling about him, wanted to cry. "Not a drinking problem. *A living problem.*"

There was a pause on the other end.

"I was wrong, Mr. Sanders," the doctor said with resignation. "It happens to the best of us."

CO-DEPENDENT ROLE IN THIS TRAP

Like most aspects of addiction, relapse is often inadvertently facilitated by the behavior of those around the alcoholic. In Melvin's case, his principal enabler is his psychiatrist, who with the best intentions undertakes to treat Melvin using what has been shown over the years to be the least effective technique for initial treatment—weekly one-to-one psychotherapy based on understanding one's childhood. To his credit, he does recommend AA, but doesn't follow up to see if Melvin is complying. He is slow to establish a dialogue with Melvin's wife, which allows Melvin to control the flow of information to and from the physician—information that forms the basis for evaluation of his progress in treatment.

This is particularly harmful because Melvin is in denial, and his view of reality is still polluted by alcohol. In the long run, the best contribution this psychiatrist can make to his patient's recovery is simply to give up. Enabling isn't only found among individuals; sometimes entire organizations "institutionalize" relapse by setting policies that effectively bar the alcoholic from the help he needs. A good example is the trend to reduce insurance benefits for addiction treatment. Though most policies provide benefits, access may be so limited that inpatient care is for all practical purposes unavailable—even for those who have failed as outpatients. The insurance company asks the doctor to demonstrate convincingly that such treatment is "medically necessary"—in other words, that the patient is too physically or psychologically ill to be treated as an outpatient. If he isn't, then they expect the doctor to discharge him and continue treatment on an outpatient basis, or they won't pay the claim.

This makes sense from that limited perspective. But the problem in treating addiction isn't simply that the patient is medically or psychiatrically ill. It's that without a certain level of intensive treatment on the front end, most addicts will *never establish stable abstinence in the first place.* So though a given patient might be medically or psychologically stable enough for outpatient care—meaning that he isn't likely to die of some other illness or take his own life—it doesn't necessarily mean he'll be able to stay off alcohol and drugs.

THE DIRECTIONS FOR INITIAL RECOVERY

To avoid or extricate yourself from this trap, you must first understand what keeps it going. That's simple: it's your insistence on doing things your own way. You've probably made *personal or psychological comfort* the measuring stick for treatment. If you're asking yourself, "How will this make me feel?" you're asking yourself the wrong question. You should be asking another, far more important question: "How do I know this will *work?*"

That's true even when you're relating stories of people who relapsed as evidence that treatment is a waste of time. Everyone knows someone who relapsed following treatment. Everyone also knows someone who didn't. You're simply reinforcing your own opinion by selectively ignoring certain evidence, and drawing conclusions that reinforce your reluctance—it's part of the nature of your disease.

So in a sense it's like a runaway locomotive: all that power and speed careening toward what must inevitably be a tragic end. To stop it, you're going to have to get someone else in the engineer's seat. Somebody who knows what he or she is doing.

Here's how. Remember: these are directions for obtaining adequate initial treatment. Follow them exactly. *Do not change one single thing.*

Step One: Find an expert.

In other words, find someone you can turn your life over to for the next few months, at least in terms of treating your addiction. This could be a treatment center, a clinic, whatever—it just has to be someone who is knowledgeable enough to give you the correct advice and explain to you why you should follow it. Because you're going to have a lot of questions.

It's not important that you *trust* this person in the same way that you trust a good friend. This isn't a good friend, any more than your oncologist would be if you had cancer. What you're looking for is expertise, delivered in such a way that you can understand what you're supposed to do.

Step Two: Get clear directions.

If he's any good, he'll want to give you a set of clear directions. Get a phone number where you can reach him when you have questions. Remember, you're going to have a lot of questions, because your brain is going to be trying to figure out how to *avoid* doing what this person has told you to do.

How do you know if these directions are any good? They should be the same ones we give in this book, in more or less the same order. Or get a second opinion from another qualified individual.

Step Three: Follow those directions.

Now comes the hard part. You're going to want to cheat. Everyone does. If you do cheat, you throw off your chances of success. Maybe you'll be the one who gets away with it. Maybe you won't.

Following directions over an extended period of time— especially if they're inconvenient or psychologically taxing—is about the most difficult thing anyone does. It's also the key to dealing with illness, because diseases respond to what people *do* more than they respond to how people *feel* about doing it.

Do the right thing. The rest will follow.

Step Four: Be patient with results.

Don't look for immediate gratification. You'll begin improving the minute you break the cycle of intoxication and withdrawal, and every time you avoid a slip where in the past you would have taken a full header off the high board, you'll make a quantum leap in your recovery. But newly recovering people tend to look only for what *hasn't* happened yet—the rewards that still haven't arrived—while ignoring the ones that have. So be patient. Time heals a lot.

AN EXERCISE WITH BRAIN TELEVISION

If the Attitude Check #1 (pages 64–65) revealed a problem with following directions, do this exercise. Remember, brain television is simply a way to make use of your innate powers of visualization to examine certain aspects of your past, present, and future experience.

Close your eyes and picture a television set. On the bottom left is a knob that regulates volume or intensity, depending on the situation. Directly below the middle of the screen is another knob, which turns the set on and off. On the bottom right-hand side is a knob for changing channels.

Turn the set on and let it warm up while you take a few slow breaths and relax. Ready? Now picture on the screen in front of you a recent incident where someone in authority was telling you to do something you didn't want to do. It could be a situation at work, at school, or in a personal relationship. Got it? Now play the scene through on the brain TV screen. Picture the room where it took place, the time of day, the expression on the face of the person you were talking with. Go through the scene mentally, just as you recall it happened.

Now take note of what was going on in your body while you thought about your interaction. Did your stomach feel tight? Were you aware of any anger? Did you have any sensation in the back of your neck? Simply take note of those sensations.

When done, allow the screen to go blank. Now think back to a previous occasion—before the episode you just relived—where you experienced a similar situation and felt much the same in response to it. Picture it on the screen. Who you were talking with. The time and place. Note the furniture, if any, in the room. Again, note the sensations in your stomach, your shoulders, the back of your neck. Don't linger more than a few seconds; don't get caught up in your feelings. They serve only as a reference point; you're not trying to "work through" some psychological issue. You're only trying to see how far back this pattern extends.

Now blank the screen, and once again think back to an even earlier occasion when you experienced the same kind of reaction. Put the image on the screen like a scene from a television show. When you've done that, blank the screen and replace it with still another scene from still another episode where you experienced these same feelings.

For most of us, it begins in childhood, and it's quite possible you'll find its origin in a scene with a parent. Keep going until you feel you have a good handle on where it comes from.

Now take a scene from childhood—the earliest one you can recall—and replay it so it comes out differently. If there was something you wanted to say, say it. Have your parent or other authority figure respond in the way you would have liked. When

you've finished, reach out with your right hand and turn the
channel changer on the lower right side of the TV set. There's a
beach scene on the screen. Imagine yourself on the beach; look
out over the ocean and take a few deep, relaxing breaths. Let the
sensations in your body dissipate: your shoulders, stomach, jaw,
neck, come to relax. When you feel good, turn off the set and
open your eyes.

FIVE THINGS YOU CAN DO TO PRACTICE FOLLOWING DIRECTIONS

1. Each day, change something about your behavior. Start with
    something simple, such as wearing your watch on the oppo-
    site wrist or putting your coat on, opposite arm first. This is
    to get you accustomed to the odd feeling that accompanies
    behavior change.
2. Buy a book on diet or nutrition for recovering people (see the
    Suggested Reading section). Follow the directions in the
    book for one to four weeks. Do you notice a tendency to
    cheat, and to rationalize it?
3. Write an "autobiography" of your life in terms of the way you
    respond to being told what to do. Use some of the incidents
    from the brain TV exercise (pages 76–78).
4. Tell your counselor or sponsor that you want to be told the
    truth about your behavior even if it makes you temporarily
    angry. Promise them that you won't hold a grudge and that
    you appreciate their honesty.
5. Every time you meet with a counselor or sponsor, ask them if
    there's anything in particular they feel you should do before
    the next time you meet. If they give you a suggestion, make
    sure you do it. If you find yourself reacting negatively to
    something they suggest, share that feeling with them. Then
    do what they suggest anyway.

THE SECOND TRAP:
THE FAILURE TO SELF-DIAGNOSE

"We admitted we were powerless over
alcohol—that our lives had become
unmanageable."

—Step One
The Twelve Steps of
Alcoholics Anonymous

Remember the four goals of treatment? The first was to learn about your disease. The second is to apply that information to yourself.

That's what motivates you to stay away from drugs and alcohol in the future. If you haven't self-diagnosed, you'll eventually relapse, no matter what else you do, because your motivation for sobriety will decrease as you feel better.

Sound confusing? Let's review it a step at a time.

When you first enter treatment—whether a formal program, a Twelve Step group, or counseling—it's almost always because of some kind of pressure. Maybe you were arrested, or threatened by the law. Perhaps you're in danger of losing your job, or getting tossed out of school. It might be that you've strained your financial resources and gone hopelessly into debt. Maybe you're suffering from withdrawal or have reached your psychological breaking point. Whether the pressure comes from outside or from the demands of the body is irrelevant. The key is that you perceive it as beyond your immediate control.

This concerted pressure produces a *window* in your denial. It isn't a very big window, but it's enough to scare you.

Let's illustrate it with a short exercise. Imagine you're driving along on a country road. A fog rolls in and begins to thicken around your vehicle, reducing your visibility to almost nothing. Just as you're about ready to give up and pull over, the fog lifts a bit. You get a glimpse of the road ahead. To your surprise, you notice you've reached a fork in the road, and you have a choice: you can continue in the direction you've been going or you can take the other route. You have a chance to decide which road you want to take. If you don't decide, however, the fog will close in again and you'll be forced to muddle along toward your original destination as best you can. The opportunity for change will have passed.

Which do you choose? Most of us—not knowing where the second road goes—reflexively continue on our way. In short order, we forget the second choice existed. After all, we can no longer see it.

This is very much like the experience of addiction. The fog represents denial, and a crisis often produces a temporary lifting of the fog—an opportunity to change direction. But all crises, whether internal or external, abate with time. Whatever pressure drove the alcoholic into treatment in the first place grows weaker by the moment. And when its emotional impact fades beyond a certain point—well, it's like the fog closing in again. The time for choosing direction is past, and you'll just have to keep going forward, toward whatever end awaits you. You won't get another opportunity to change until the next break in the fog (usually another crisis).

In addiction, the first road is a return to active drug use, and the second path is that of self-diagnosis. It's the point at which you look at your own experience and decide that you suffer from a chronic disease. Moreover, you realize your disease can and will *kill* you if you don't do something about it—a revelation that spurs you to change.

This is the source of motivation. It took treatment professionals an inordinately long time to discover that. Counselors struggled to develop techniques and instruments for assessing motivation, as though it were some sort of fuel and you could measure it with a gas gauge. But motivation is usually founded on a simple belief: that you have a potentially fatal disease which you can, if you work at it, survive.

If you believe this, you'll strive toward recovery. Conversely, if you don't believe it, then you won't. As the crisis passes and pressure eases, motivation will seem to drain away like fuel from a leaky tank. Relapse will follow.

Thus, the second common reason for treatment failure is a failure to self-diagnose. How could anyone go through an intensive treatment program without recognizing their own illness? It's simple: this is the realm where the alcoholic has centered most of his defenses. *It isn't easy for someone in denial to realize they suffer from a chronic disease.* There are a number of obstacles in the way.

These obstacles generally take the form of *objections:* aspects of your experience that to you seem to indicate that your problems are caused by something other than addiction.

ATTITUDE CHECK #2: SELF-DIAGNOSIS

To find out how easy it will be for you to self-diagnose, answer yes or no to the following statements. A word of advice: be honest. Nobody's looking over your shoulder.

1. I feel that in many ways I am very different from most people who have alcohol or drug problems.
2. I don't feel like I fit in a Twelve Step meeting.
3. In the past, I've been able to control my use of alcohol or drugs. That makes me wonder whether I was really addicted.
4. Even now, there are periods where I can drink or use drugs without getting into trouble.
5. I feel that the problems that brought me to treatment were not entirely my fault.

6. I know people who drink or use more than I do, and they aren't in trouble.

7. I feel my problems are due more to my difficulties with other people than to my drug or alcohol use.

8. Even though I recognize the need to give up some drugs, I believe that there are others I could safely use.

9. I feel I've learned my lesson, and I will never allow myself to get in trouble with drugs or alcohol again.

10. I hear people at AA meetings talk about things that have never happened to me. I feel they're a lot worse than I am.

11. I'm happy I caught my problem early.

12. I wonder if I can be an alcoholic when I've never had a blackout or been arrested.

13. I wonder if I was really an addict, because I didn't use every day.

14. I wonder if I really need treatment. I feel I could have stopped on my own.

15. I suspect that someday I'll be able to return to social drinking.

16. I feel that my real problem was psychological, and that the drugs and alcohol were just a symptom.

17. I suspect that my biggest problem is the lack of support I get from people around me.

18. I believe that the main reason I used drugs or alcohol was out of boredom.

19. I think that addiction is really a response to stress.

20. I do not believe that addiction is a disease.

Look at the box on the next page for an interpretation of the results.

If you answered "yes" to one or two of the questions your chance of relapse is low. If you answered "yes" to three or four of the questions your chance of relapse is moderate and you should continue to learn and be aware of the pitfalls of recovery. If you answered "yes" to five or six of the questions you are at high risk for relapse and should pay particular attention to this trap. If you answered "yes" to seven or more of the questions you are in a relapse "red zone" and need to seek and follow good advice immediately.

HOW THE TRAP CLOSES

Once again, a "trap" depends on hidden assumptions that set the stage for a series of bad decisions and resultant errors in action. Each mistake seems to lead naturally to the next. In this trap, the sequence is roughly as follows:

The underlying assumption: Though in treatment, you do not self-diagnose as suffering from a chronic, progressive, and potentially fatal disease. Instead, you conclude that your problems are situational in origin.

Resulting behavior: You focus on psychosocial problems instead of disease.

The second decision: Your problems—including loss of control over alcohol or drugs—will go away with a change in your situation.

Resulting behavior: You lose interest in addictions treatment, and concentrate on changing your environment.

The third decision: Having decided that you do not have addictive disease, you "compare out" with other people at Twelve Step groups or in treatment—you become an "outsider."

Resulting behavior: You stop attending meetings and counseling sessions.

The fourth decision: You reason that since you are not alcoholic or addicted, an occasional drink or drug is not going to hurt you, if you're careful.

Resulting behavior: Reintroduction of the drug.

RED FLAGS

This is often the pattern of the "white-knuckle" alcoholic, uncomfortable in sobriety, waiting for a probationary period to pass so that he can use the drug again. People will probably comment on your continued defensiveness and the extent to which you focus on outside problems. In some cases, you'll be nearly as defensive about addiction when abstinent as when under the influence of drugs.

Here again are the thoughts and phrases that serve as warning flags that you are about to tumble into this relapse trap.

1. "I don't think I'm really like all these other people. My situation is different, because I'm (better advantaged, less advantaged, et cetera)."
2. "I never (got arrested, had medical problems, got fired, lost my family, et cetera), so I don't think my problem is as bad as most."
3. "My difficulties were really due to (worry, overwork, grief, stress, depression, emotional crisis, et cetera) that was going on in my life at the time."
4. "If I hadn't been (careless, distracted, under pressure, overwhelmed, angry, depressed, anxious, et cetera), I never would have allowed things to get to this point."
5. "It's (his, her, their) fault."
6. "Well, it wasn't as bad as they made it seem, anyway."

RELAPSE IN ACTION

Mandy Wilson for the Defense

Mandy, a defense attorney by profession, is now a patient in a treatment program. She has a very serious cocaine problem, and the program was selected after considerable study by her employer and her family. They chose this program based on its clinical reputation, its beautiful setting, and its proximity to her home. It costs a great deal of money, and everyone who has been touched by Mandy's addiction—her boss, her mom and dad, her longtime fiancé, her nine-year-old daughter, even her ex-husband—fervently hopes it will be successful.

Unfortunately, it won't. Mandy is going to relapse. It may not happen for several months, but sooner or later, she will resume cocaine use. There'll be what the psychologists call a "precipitating factor," something that goes wrong in her life and seems to motivate her relapse—a personal crisis or professional setback—but that will serve only to obscure issues. In reality, Mandy's relapse began the day she entered treatment. She's about to complete an expensive, intensive treatment program without accomplishing its most important task. She will fail to recognize that she has a disease.

In some respects, she might as well have taken a cruise, or stayed home in bed, for all the good treatment is going to do her.

Let's look in as Mandy begins to fail. Here she is as she relates her drug history to her physician.

MANDY: I think maybe I should clarify a few things. In the first place, I never used much marijuana in school. Less than most of my friends. And drinking was just, you know, purely teenage rebellion. I was the straight one in the bunch.

PHYSICIAN: So what's your point?

MANDY: Just that I don't want you to get the wrong impression. My problem didn't really start until I was hanging around with musicians. Coke was everywhere. I would have been a social outcast if I hadn't at least tried it.

Mandy is *minimizing* her previous drug history in order to convince the interviewer (and herself) that her problem is relatively recent in origin. She then *rationalizes* her use as a response to peer pressure.

PHYSICIAN: But you didn't stop with experimentation.

MANDY: No, that's true. But I know what a cocaine addict is, and believe me, I don't qualify. I have some stories about my musician clients that would make your eyes pop. People staying awake for weeks at a time, getting paranoid, threatening people with guns . . . By their standards, I was strictly minor league.

PHYSICIAN: Still, your own use was heavy. You must have known something was wrong.

MANDY: It was just more than I wanted. I was spending money on it—although not that much. I didn't like what it was doing to me. And I wanted to stop it.

PHYSICIAN: Why did you wait until you wore a hole in your nasal septum and had to have surgery?

MANDY: Now wait a minute, my nose wasn't entirely due to the drugs. There were other factors. The surgeon told me I had some tissue deterioration. I remember he said that it could be caused by things like poor diet, which I feel was a factor because I was working an eighty-hour week and trying to lose weight, and I just wasn't eating right.

PHYSICIAN: So you don't feel you were out of control?

MANDY: Well, it depends on what you mean by out of control. I believe I could have stopped myself at any time, if I chose to. But because of a combination of circumstances, I didn't. I think if I'd gotten a little more cooperation from people, I would have quit by myself, eventually. But your friends are never there when you want them. They're always more than ready to tell you how to run your life, though. There are a lot of volunteers for that job.

This is a good illustration of four distinct defense mechanisms. First, Mandy *intellectualizes,* arguing definitions (Who is a cocaine addict? for example) rather than addressing the question directly. Then she reveals specific *denial* around the issue of loss of control (see the section entitled "The Third Trap: Experimenting With Control," beginning on p. 99), insisting that she could have stopped at any time, but didn't want to. She then *externalizes* her problems onto other people. It's the old "if you had to put up with you, you'd be a drug addict, too" defense.

PHYSICIAN: Mandy, do you believe you were addicted to cocaine? Or alcohol, or marijuana, or tranquilizers?

MANDY: Absolutely not. Of course, it depends on how you define addiction. I didn't use it every day. I would quit for days at a time. Most of the time, I was in control of it.

Here, she is *comparing out*—pointing to symptoms she doesn't have as proof she isn't addicted, while ignoring those she has experienced. She assumes that if she doesn't have all the symptoms, she doesn't have the disease. That's an erroneous (and dangerous) assumption. The symptoms of progressive disease tend to multiply over time.

Three weeks later, prior to discharge, Mandy is having a similar conversation.

PHYSICIAN: So, Mandy, I see you've enrolled in the aftercare program. That's good.

MANDY: Oh, yes. Well, it's very inconvenient, but it will probably be a condition of retaining my license. But I made my bed, and now I'll have to sleep in it, won't I?

PHYSICIAN: How do you feel about your experience here?

MANDY: Well, I feel I've learned a lot, although I could have done as well on my own. I guess it wouldn't have looked as good to the bar counsel, however . . . and it was good to get away from the stress for a few weeks. I realize now that I was exhausted. Dealing with work, and my kid, is a pain in the ass, sometimes . . . I just wish they hadn't dragged my parents into this, because I think it put them through a lot of needless worry. I had a problem, but I know I would have done something about it, given time . . . I just didn't know what was the best way to deal with it. But that's all water under the bridge.

As you can see, Mandy's attitude is essentially unchanged. She still externalizes the causes of her addiction. She still downplays her drug use in comparison to work and family problems. She continues to resent her family's involvement. She complies with treatment only to avoid the specific consequence that brought her to the program.

PHYSICIAN: Mandy, I suppose the counselors have told you they have misgivings about your prognosis. They think you're not very motivated to stay sober.

MANDY: Oh, yeah, I've heard that before. And to be perfectly honest, I can't believe they let people who haven't even got a college degree work in treatment programs. So what if they're recovering alcoholics? That doesn't mean they have the qualifications to tell other people how to live their lives.

PHYSICIAN: Well, what about me? Do I have the necessary qualifications?

MANDY: Of course, don't be ridiculous. You're a psychiatrist.

PHYSICIAN: I suspect you're not as motivated as we'd like you to be, either.

MANDY: Would you mind explaining that?

PHYSICIAN: Basically, it's three things. First, you're not saying you're an addict. Or rather, when you do say it, you don't sound like you mean it.

MANDY: I just don't feel my addiction was as bad as people make it out to be. There's a difference.

PHYSICIAN: Second, when you talk about aftercare, you make it sound like a condition of probation rather than your own choice.

MANDY: No, I want to go. I would have done it on my own. That's what is so crazy about this whole thing: you people are telling me to do things I would do anyway. And because it all happened to come to a head before I had a chance to take action, everybody assumes I'm resisting it.

PHYSICIAN: And third, I'm not convinced you identify with the people at NA.

MANDY: Sure I do. I'm no better than they are, except maybe socially and educationally. But I don't look down on them.

Confrontation does little to shake Mandy's opinion of herself. The flaws in her logic will become weak points in her recovery plan. By minimizing the severity of her addiction, she removes her motive for working at staying sober. By insisting that she would have recovered without help, she justifies dropping out of her aftercare program a few weeks or months from now. By "comparing out" with others in her Twelve Step group, she sets herself up to terminate that involvement as well.

One thing Mandy doesn't lack is confidence. Listen to her final pronouncement.

PHYSICIAN: So you feel you're going to do well.

MANDY: As far as using cocaine? I'm absolutely sure I'm not going to use it again. I'd be crazy to go back, after coming all this way. It's the other stuff in my life that's going to be the problem. Work and being a mother and everything. What I really need is a new life [she smiles] . . . but the drug thing—I feel I have a handle on that."

CO-DEPENDENT ROLE IN THIS TRAP

Family and friends are often so relieved that the alcoholic is finally in a treatment program that they unwittingly play right into the comparing-out process. For example, we've had numerous examples of family members approaching the program staff to make requests on behalf of the patient—one wife asked that we allow her husband's secretary to set up a desk and computer terminal in his room so that he could conduct "essential business" while confined for twenty-one days. Her rationale: she was so grateful he'd at long last agreed to treatment that she felt compelled to do everything in her power to make it as painless as possible. We turned down her request, of course. It hadn't occurred to her that if he spent the entire three weeks conducting business, he'd never get around to learning about alcoholism, and thus would waste his time and money.

Part of the problem is that family members sometimes equate comfort with success. The family reasons that the addict must be comfortable with the treatment process in order to benefit. But self-diagnosis depends not at all on psychological or physical comfort. It is contingent upon recognizing some rather painful truths about one's situation. In some respects, someone who is too comfortable is least likely to acknowledge the need for change.

It's also important to remember that addictions treatment is built around the notion that all victims of alcoholism and drug dependency have quite a bit in common. So it isn't helpful for friends or family members to keep reinforcing the idea that every addict is unique. Human beings are unique, and treatment makes no effort to deny that. But alcoholism takes people of all different ages, backgrounds, personalities, and aspirations, and makes them behave in remarkably similar ways. Having the family act as the alcoholic's emissary to the treatment professional sets up two false expectations: first, that the family will continue to serve as "protector" for the alcoholic, and second, that the addict is not responsible for negotiating his own settlements with the world. Both are counterproductive.

Physicians and psychiatrists are often tremendous enablers in this respect, because they, too, tend to treat their patients as different from everyone else. This is especially true where a patient has been in psychotherapy for an extended period before the psychiatrist realized he was dealing with alcoholism or drug dependency. Patient and psychiatrist may already have spent a great deal of time recalling and analyzing childhood experiences, and it's nearly impossible to make an intellectual leap from this to the awareness of an underlying disease process. Thus the psychiatrist may find himself explaining the patient's behavior in terms of those same childhood experiences, and might be reluctant to make a recommendation for alcoholism treatment for fear of "contaminating" their relationship. This in turn can set up two false expectations in the mind of the patient: first, that solving outside problems is the key to abstinence (it isn't), and second, that insight into those childhood forces might eventually restore the ability to drink or use drugs. Both

run counter to the process of self-diagnosis and the prospects of
recovery.

HOW TO AVOID THIS TRAP

Let's do this in three steps. First, we'll learn the definitions of
some important terms. Then, we'll apply that information to
our own experience so we can identify any signs or symptoms of
the disease. Finally, we'll make a list of objections to self-
diagnosis and answer each of them.

Step One

Turn to the glossary in the back of this book. Learn the definitions of the following terms:

Tolerance

Withdrawal

Blackout

Loss of control

Compulsive use

Organ deterioration

Continued use despite adverse consequences

Got it? If you don't understand any of the definitions or
have questions, discuss them with a knowledgeable person
before you begin this next exercise. When you're ready, proceed.

Step Two: A brain TV exercise

Turn on your brain television. Remember you have a control
knob on the left that adjusts the volume and the intensity. And
on the right you have a channel changer.

Blank the screen. Now, let's put a word across the screen, like the title of an episode of your favorite show, which is, of course, *This Is Your Life*. The word we're putting across the screen is, in capital letters, TOLERANCE.

You know what tolerance is. It's the ability to consume larger than normal amounts of alcohol without obvious intoxication. Or if you're using another drug, it's easier to think of it as the need to use more to get the same effect.

Okay, now form a picture on the screen. A picture of yourself, when you were drinking or using drugs, discovering that the effect was wearing off and you needed more. Did you ever experience a point where you felt like the drugs could no longer get you high—that you'd reached a "ceiling" beyond which you couldn't go? Note how you feel. Is there any panic there? Any sense of frustration?

Got that picture? Okay. Now think of the time previous to that episode when you felt something similar. When you experienced the same feeling.

Got it? Now, go to the time before the last episode, when you experienced the same or a similar feeling.

Don't tarry long. Just take note of the feeling and of the circumstances of that particular episode. If the intensity of the feeling gets too great, use the volume knob to decrease it. Or if you prefer, turn the sound off completely and just watch the silent picture.

Keep going back until you think you're about to the point where you first experienced that feeling. Pay more attention to that episode. Where were you? Who were you with? How old were you? Approximately what year was it? What was your response?

When you're done, turn off the TV, and when you're ready open your eyes. Take a piece of paper and a pen and write out a brief synopsis of your history in regards to this particular symptom. Describe in more detail the first episode.

Now let your eyes fall closed. When you're ready, turn on your brain television, and let a new title form on the screen: LOSS OF CONTROL. Repeat the process. Think of the last time when you drank or used more than you intended. Remember how that felt. Do you have the sense of it?

Got the picture? Now think back to the time before that when you experienced a similar feeling: that you had consumed more chemicals than you really wanted to. Keep going, using that feeling as a reference point, until you come to the point where you feel you are near the first experience with loss of control. Again, if at any time the feeling grows too intense, then simply adjust the volume knob to reduce it. After all, this is only a TV show. Turn it off if you want.

When you reach that earliest point, pay special attention to the circumstances of that episode. Where were you? Who were you with? How old were you? What year was it? Who else was important to you at that time in your life? What were you thinking?

When you're done, turn off the TV, let your eyes open, and make notes on your paper as you did in the first part of the exercise.

Continue until you've completed four symptoms, or until you need a break. For example, when you examine the phenomenon of BLACKOUTS, use the feeling of not being able to remember something you did or said as a reference point. When you study COMPULSIVE USE, look at the feeling of needing more and more and still not being satisfied. When you experience CONTINUED USE DESPITE ADVERSE CONSEQUENCES, examine the feeling of being scared of what will happen—getting sick, getting hurt, getting caught, et cetera—and going ahead and doing the drug anyway. Go back through all the episodes where you experienced this feeling.

These feelings are the *reference points* for the exercise. They are what tie these episodes together in your memory. It doesn't matter how intensely you feel them; that isn't relevant at this point. They are just a way of remembering things that you might otherwise have forgotten. If the feeling becomes painful, simply let it pass. Or adjust the volume knob. There's no need to hurt.

Step Three

When you're done with all the symptoms—this can be done slowly, over several weeks—then write out an essay entitled "How I Know I Have a Disease and Must Abstain." Use episodes from this exercise to illustrate your point.

Share this with a counselor, a sponsor, and another knowledgeable person. Get their feedback.

SOME COMMON OBJECTIONS TO SELF-DIAGNOSIS

There are as many objections to recognizing that you're an alcoholic as there are bottles of whiskey in the world. Here are just a few—and our answers. Do any seem familiar?

1. I feel that in many ways I am very different from most people who have alcohol or drug problems.

    No two alcoholics or addicts are exactly alike. But they have a great deal in common—for instance, the experience of a disease.
2. I don't feel like I fit in at Twelve Step meetings.

    Twelve Step groups are made up of people. You fit in at least as well as you do when you're at the local mall or waiting in line at the bank. In fact, if you've had a problem with alcohol and drugs, you fit in a lot better.
3. In the past, I've been able to control my use of alcohol or drugs. That makes me wonder whether I was really addicted.

Alcoholics and addicts spend years "controlling" their drug use. It seldom occurs to them that the need to deliberately control consumption of a drug is indicative of mounting dependence. As time passes, the periods of control grow less frequent, and evidence of loss of control more obvious.

4. Even now, there are periods where I can drink or use drugs without getting into trouble.

Of course there are. But once you reach the late stages, there won't be. Think back: Is your problem worse than it was, say, five years ago?

5. I feel that the problems that brought me to treatment were not entirely my fault.

They never are. But don't underestimate the extent to which the cycle of intoxication and withdrawal can change the way you think, act, and feel. Perhaps you would have been able to *avoid* these problems had you not been in trouble with drugs.

6. I know people who drink or use more than I do, and they aren't in trouble.

You also know people who are sicker than you are who aren't dead. Does that make you immune from dying?

7. I feel my problems are due more to my difficulties with other people than to my drug or alcohol use.

You've learned to focus your attention on the behavior of others rather than yourself. You *situationalize* your difficulties, refusing to see the larger pattern. Perhaps you're a bit like the young man who was confronted by his lawyer. "You've been arrested five times in the last four years for drug possession," the attorney said. "What do you think that means?" The defendant thought for a moment. "I'm unlucky," he replied.

8. Even though I recognize the need to give up some drugs, I believe that there are others I could safely use.

The addict's search for a "safe" drug is a little like the

alchemist's search for the formula to turn stone into gold. In NA, they call it "research," as in "Try it, and come back to us if you aren't successful."

9. I feel I've learned my lesson, and I will never allow myself to get in trouble with drugs or alcohol again.

This vow might work if your problem was just that you were ignorant. But it's no match for withdrawal or loss of control.

10. I hear people at AA meetings talk about things that have never happened to me. I feel they're a lot worse than I am.

Some of them undoubtedly are. Others would probably be frightened if they listened to *your* story. *Golly,* they'd think, *I'm glad I didn't let it get that far!*

11. I'm happy I caught my problem early.

You didn't. Nobody ever does. People come into treatment because they have entered the difficult middle stage of the disease. Where are the early-stage alcoholics and addicts? Drinking and using drugs, of course.

12. I wonder if I can be an alcoholic when I've never had a blackout or been arrested.

This is "comparing out." About 50% of alcoholics do not experience blackouts. Only a minority of addicts and alcoholics will be arrested.

13. I wonder if I was really an addict, because I didn't use every day.

Most addicts don't use every day, especially if they have trouble obtaining drugs. An exception might be a maintenance alcoholic, a narcotics addict, or somebody with good access to chemicals. Some get around the problem of availability by alternating drugs depending on the supply.

14. I wonder if I really need treatment. I feel I could have stopped on my own.

Astonishingly, most alcoholics and addicts who enter

treatment believe they don't "really" need it, despite their many previous failures. Remember: the problem isn't stopping: it's staying stopped.

15. I suspect that someday I'll be able to return to social drinking.

The alcoholic's equivalent of the drug addict's search for the "safe" drug (see question 8). If that were possible, you probably would never have arrived in treatment.

16. I feel my real problem was psychological, and the drugs and alcohol were just a symptom.

This is an expression of the psychodynamic model (see page 51). It tends to shift focus away from addiction and toward personality issues. The problem: it's extremely difficult (if not impossible) to change your personality. You could die of alcoholism before you do.

17. I suspect that my biggest problem is the lack of support I get from people around me.

This is an expression of the family systems model (see page 54). The assumption: if other people were more supportive, you wouldn't need alcohol or drugs. In reality, most alcoholics and addicts suffer from *too much support* from others—that's called "enabling."

18. I believe that the main reason I used drugs or alcohol is out of boredom.

Boredom is a motive to drink or get stoned—like stress, peer pressure, and the desire to socialize. It does not, however, explain addiction, any more than hunger explains compulsive overeating.

19. I think that addiction is really a response to stress.

This is an expression of the wet moral model (see page 47) or the behaviorist model (see page 52). The principal cause of stress in the lives of most alcoholics and addicts is alcoholism and drug addiction. Eliminate that, and you'll be surprised at how much else you can handle.

20. I do not believe that addiction is a disease.

You probably aren't sure about the definition of disease. Here it is: *a morbid process with characteristic identifying symptoms, whether the etiology* (cause) *or prognosis* (outcome) *is known or unknown.* That's very broad, isn't it? Clearly, alcoholism qualifies. What you're really saying is that you think alcoholism is "less" of a disease than cancer or pneumonia or hypertension. But that doesn't alter the fact that it fits the definition.

THE THIRD TRAP: EXPERIMENTING WITH CONTROL

"I realized I didn't really want 'a' cigarette—I wanted all the cigarettes in the world, one after another. The first was just a way to get at the rest."

—a former smoker

Denial pervades addiction. But there's a very peculiar and persistent denial that surrounds the issue of abstinence.

Perhaps this is why AA's First Step suggests you admit you are powerless over alcohol rather than simply that you are an alcoholic. In many people's minds, they're not the same thing.

We learned this the hard way. Like most, our treatment program makes extensive use of recovering volunteers. One of our best was a grandmotherly lady named Billie. Married to an equally grandparently fellow named Wally, she claimed some eight years of sobriety within AA.

In addition to being the ideal volunteer, Billie was equally active in AA. So you can imagine how surprised we were one Saturday night to find Billie in the detox ward—*as a patient.*

Since she was unconscious, we asked Wally what had gone wrong. He shrugged.

"Who knows? Every so often she just . . ." He trailed off.

"We were under the impression she'd been sober for many years," we said. "You make it sound like this has happened more recently."

He looked puzzled. "Almost a year ago. That was the last binge. She's been fine otherwise. Maybe a few drinks a week, but nothing more."

We were stunned. "You mean to tell us Billie never stopped drinking?"

Wally looked insulted. "Of course she stopped drinking. I just told you she only drinks a couple of times a year."

"No, you said she has a few drinks every week."

"That's what I said. Since she stopped drinking, she just has a few drinks a week."

"Wally, let's clear this up. When you say Billie stopped drinking, you mean she's cut back to a few drinks a week. You don't mean she's totally abstinent."

He was getting mad now. "She's totally abstinent. She's not drinking vodka and falling asleep at the dinner table and stumbling around the house and throwing up in the toilet. She's *not drinking.* The only time she even gets near alcohol is when she has a cocktail or two before dinner. And that's not even two days in a row."

Gradually it dawned on us that in Wally's mind, "drinking" meant a binge, and "not drinking" meant controlled consumption.

We'd put a lot of trust in Billie and felt more than a little betrayed. So when she awoke the next morning, we went to see her.

"Billie," we said, "you go to AA three times a week. Would you please tell us how you reconcile that with drinking?"

You could see she thought this was a silly question.

"Oh, I realized a long time ago," she said, "that AA's definition of sobriety would always be different from mine."

Somewhere, buried deep in the psyche of every addict, is the conviction that one more drink, joint, hit, or shot wouldn't hurt. *As long as I stopped there,* you think, *what harm could it bring?* The problem is that even though "one drink" is not in itself terribly damaging, the addict's nature is to go back for more.

Remember that addictive disease is characterized as a compulsive disorder. You probably know this as "the potato chip syndrome." Normally, the best way to stop a craving is to satisfy it. But a compulsion interrupts this process: giving in to your craving actually causes it to increase. You find yourself wanting more and more, perhaps to the point where you've made yourself physically ill. Alcoholics Anonymous sums this up in a proverb: "One is too many, and a thousand is not enough."

Most addicts learn this through bitter experience. Suppose your intention is to confine yourself to two beers. But once you start, you discover that something impairs your ability to stop. You keep going until you're way over the limit. Being drunk, you do or say something that makes you look ridiculous and other people angry.

Later on, you reflect on the episode. You probably don't question the merits of drinking. After all, you already possess a vast fund of experience that tells you that drinking is intrinsically good. Rather you ask yourself, At what point did I lose control? Was it with the third drink, that magic line which I've heard "moderate" drinkers never cross? Or with the fifth, when my speech began to slur a tiny bit and my hand began to waver? Or even the seventh, since I once read an article that said that "heavy drinkers" consumed more than six ounces a day?

Of course, this is like sitting around trying to figure out which potato chip makes you want the next one. But it's serious business not only to alcoholics but to researchers, who spent many years designing behavior-modification programs based on learning to recognize the precise point at which loss of control began. The point where, they imagined, "social" drinking passed over the line into alcoholism.

Some alcoholics become obsessed with this issue. As loss of control progresses, they engage in a titanic struggle to assert their will over the disease. Each failure brings another vow to succeed with the next attempt. *Maybe this time,* they tell themselves, *things will be different.*

In response, AA developed its suggestion of total abstinence. It's a practical rather than a moral imperative. The early members of AA finally broke through to the shining truth that if you didn't have the first one, you couldn't have the second. And that's what we teach people in the great majority of modern treatment programs.

Still, not everybody listens. Some people remain charter members of what AA calls its "research division": those who are still trying to regain control over alcohol and drugs.

ATTITUDE CHECK #3: EXPERIMENTS WITH CONTROL

To find out whether or not you're still holding on to the idea of controlled consumption answer yes or no to the following statements.

1. I believe that I drank or used drugs for psychological reasons.
2. I was never *physically* addicted to alcohol or drugs.
3. I suspect many recovering alcoholics have a drink from time to time, even if they don't get caught.
4. I believe some alcoholics can safely return to drinking.
5. I believe that some recovering addicts can use certain

drugs—marijuana or alcohol, for example—without returning to heroin, cocaine, or something worse.

6. I feel that I could have gotten away with more drinking or drug use except for the problems it caused for other people.

7. I feel that when I drank too much or went on a binge, it was principally because of the particular situation I found myself in at the time.

8. It's hard for me to understand how *one drink* could hurt.

9. Except for my drinking or drug use, I regard myself as an exceptionally strong-willed person.

10. Whenever I've put my mind to something I've been able to accomplish it.

Look at the box below for an interpretation of the results.

> If you answered "yes" to one or two of the questions your chance of relapse is low. If you answered "yes" to three or four of the questions your chance of relapse is moderate and you should continue to learn and be aware of the pitfalls of recovery. If you answered "yes" to five or six of the questions you are at high risk for relapse and should pay particular attention to this trap. If you answered "yes" to seven or more of the questions you are in a relapse "red zone" and need to seek and follow good advice immediately.

HOW THE TRAP CLOSES

The emotional tone that surrounds this trap is one of *superficial cooperation masking quiet resistance*—or compliance without acceptance. Because this hidden agenda would be challenged should it come to light, the drinker or drug user surrounds it with secrecy.

The underlying assumption: That loss of control begins somewhere *after* the first use. This is made easier if the alcoholic assumes that addiction is caused by psychological rather than physiological factors.

Resulting behavior: The appearance of "selective" denial. You acknowledge the diagnosis of alcoholism or drug dependency and admit its adverse effects. You retain (often secretly) the belief that someday you will regain, through insight or an effort of will, the ability to drink or use certain drugs without problems. Those around you mistakenly assume you are committed to abstinence.

The second decision: You convince yourself that unlike most addicts or alcoholics, you will be able to regain control over a drug. You seek out reports that indicate this is possible.

Resulting behavior: You separate yourself from other alcoholics— first in your thinking, then physically by reducing your attendance at meetings.

The third decision: Since most alcoholics in AA are of the type that can't regain control, and wouldn't understand those who can, you decide you don't belong there.

Resulting behavior: You compare out and remain isolated at treatment activities. Though you will attend meetings if required, you get nothing out of the experience.

The fourth decision: That other people are unable to understand that you are different than the typical addict or alcoholic, and thus would attempt to impose their own misguided values on you should they know you plan to resume drinking or drug use.

Resulting behavior: You make secret plans to experiment with drinking or drugs in carefully selected, controlled situations.

The fifth decision: You interpret any successful attempt—where you use alcohol or drugs without immediate loss of control or return to other substances—as evidence that your original hypothesis was correct. And that further experiments would be justified.

Resulting behavior: More experiments. Over time, the experiments with alcohol or drugs grow more frequent and longer in duration. Eventually, loss of control occurs.

RED FLAGS

Be on the alert for the following phrases if they begin to creep into your thinking or conversation:

1. "I can't imagine that *one drink* (hit, joint, dose) would harm me."
2. "I know most alcoholics (addicts) can't drink. But some can. How do I know I'm not one of them?"
3. "I drank (used drugs) once, just to see what would happen. It wasn't any big deal. I think maybe something changed while I was sober. I think that now that I understand myself, I won't need the drug the way I used to."
4. "Other people can drink. It isn't fair."
5. "I just can't understand why I have such a problem with alcohol or drugs. I'm usually so disciplined."

RELAPSES IN ACTION

Mary Visits the Emergency Room

We'll illustrate this pattern with two examples. In the first, we see an addict exhibiting the thinking characteristic of this trap.

Mary, age 26, has just reported to an emergency room for help with her drug problem. A counselor from the detox unit has been called down to talk with her.

The counselor enters the small conference room where Mary waits. She is crying.

"Calm down, calm down. Want some Kleenex?"

Mary shakes her head. "I have some. I'm sorry to blubber like this. I must look awful."

"Don't worry. This isn't a beauty pageant." The counselor settles back in his chair. "So, what brings you to the Good Hope Emergency Room in the middle of the night?"

"I'm all screwed up on cocaine and booze."

"Ah, ha. Well, you're in luck. I'm the all-screwed-up-on-cocaine-and-booze man."

She smiles. "You don't recognize me, do you?"

"Afraid not. Should I?"

"I was here a year ago. I weighed about thirty pounds more than I do now."

He scratches his chin. "I don't suppose you lost the weight through a structured, nutritionally sound program of dietary control and behavior modification."

Mary laughs. "More like freebasing every day for about two months."

"I see. Well, when you were here before, did you go through the treatment program?"

Mary nods. "And the aftercare. I did real well, too. For about three or four months."

"Not too awfully long, is it? What happened?"

"Nothing in particular. Things were going all right. Not terrific, but basically okay, I guess. I had some cravings, but it wasn't like I was thinking about the drug all the time."

"So why did you start using?" he asks.

"I was just curious to see if . . . well, you know . . . if I could do a little bit of it and stop."

"I thought you said you were a cocaine addict."

"Oh, definitely. I know I'm an addict. No doubt in my mind. I guess I wanted to see if . . . I thought maybe I could stick with a couple of lines. Not smoking it or anything. And then stop."

"You thought as long as you didn't smoke it you would be able to stop?"

"Well, since I had only really lost control after I switched from snorting it to smoking . . . and since I used to be able to snort a few lines every now and then without going on . . . and because I'd been off it for a while . . ."

"In other words, you were hoping you could get away with it."

She nods vigorously. "Yeah. I mean, I know I'm an addict, I know I can't smoke it, I know I can't buy more than a gram at a time . . ."

"Yet you believed that if you stayed away from freebasing, snorted the stuff, used somebody else's cocaine, and didn't purchase a large quantity at any given time, you'd be able to get away with using it?"

"Yes," she says.

The counselor sits forward, fixes her gaze with his own. "My question is, Why bother? You already know what could happen. Why take the risk?"

Mary thinks for a moment. "Well, you don't like to think that you're too weak to handle something . . . I know they say it's a disease, but even then, I think you should be able to have a little self-control . . . and besides, I've been off it for a while. How do I know something hasn't changed? That is, unless I'm willing to test it."

Although Mary openly acknowledges both her addiction and her previous loss of control, she still seeks a way to conquer the disease instead of surrendering to it. It's a perfect example of *selective* denial, as well as an illustration of the "war within."

Brad Talks With the Counselor

Now let's look at someone caught in a cycle of *chronic* relapse. Brad has been treated for cocaine addiction three times, once in a special program for relapse prevention. Each time, he relapsed. Finally, following yet another relapse, a counselor interviews him.

COUNSELOR: I give up, Brad. I've tried everything I can think of, and you keep failing. We've tried every drug to suppress craving, we've got you at meetings every spare minute, we've got your whole family in therapy. And you actually seem to be doing pretty well, except every so often, you relapse. What do you think we're doing wrong?

BRAD: I don't know. Believe me, I'm as frustrated as you are. It just seems like every time I get a couple of months under my belt, something happens and I blow it.

COUNSELOR: Do you have any ideas? Anything to try next?

BRAD: No. I'm at my wit's end.

COUNSELOR: So am I. Well, Brad, why don't we call a halt to treatment? I mean, what's the point?

BRAD: What are you talking about? You can't give up on me now. I've got a lot at stake here. I'm on probation. I could lose my security clearance if I'm not in treatment. My job would dry up and blow away. I've got a family to support.

COUNSELOR: Look, I'm sorry. It just seems like whatever we're doing, it isn't working. You're not getting better.

BRAD: I can't believe you're saying that. I'm making progress! The family therapist says I'm getting in touch with my feelings. I'm getting along with my wife now, and I'm not missing work. And even though I know I'm still relapsing, each time, it feels like the urge is getting weaker . . .

Counselor: Wait a second. What urge?

Brad: The urge to do coke.

Counselor: I don't understand.

Brad: It's simple. I'm not overwhelmed with this urge to keep going until I'm out. I can start and stop, at least for a while. It's almost like when I was first using, although after a few hours, the urge comes back.

Counselor: And then what?

Brad: Then I go off, of course. I just keep using till I'm out. Till I'm completely wasted.

Counselor: Brad, are you trying to quit cocaine?

Brad: Of course. What do you mean?

Counselor: Would you like to be able to use coke again?

Brad: No. Well, of course I would, *anybody* would, if he could, it's a great drug. There's nothing in the world like it. Or at least, the first taste is terrific.

Counselor: I think I found the problem.

Brad: What?

Counselor: The reason you keep relapsing. You're not trying to quit. You want to learn how to stop after one hit.

Brad: That's crazy! I know I have to stop. Why do you think I come to all these groups and family stuff and everything?

Counselor: Because you're afraid of what will happen if you don't. You're not stupid, Brad. You know that left to your own devices you'll get in trouble. But underneath that, I think, you're hoping to get back in control. To become a social user.

BRAD: Look, I won't lie to you, of course I'd like to be able to do that. Who wouldn't? But that doesn't mean I'm planning to use it.

Brad can't see the contradiction in his own thinking. He's unaware that his desire to regain control is undermining his resolve to abstain from drugs.

COUNSELOR: Here's your problem, Brad. You think you lose control with the second line, the second pipe. Not the first.

BRAD: It sounds so unlikely.

COUNSELOR: Fits, though. Treatment doesn't work for you because you're shooting for the wrong goal. You're trying to restore control—trying, in a way, to cure your disease. Well, you're coming to the wrong place, man. Because we don't have the cure.

CO-DEPENDENT ROLE IN THIS TRAP

Family members sometimes go through a period where they suspect the alcoholic or addict is drinking or using drugs again, but they make no effort to intervene or seek help, until there are obvious signs of loss of control (drunkenness, stealing money, et cetera). When questioned later, they say that even though they were pretty sure the drug use had resumed, they couldn't see any problems associated with it, and thought that maybe this time things would be different.

Employers also may suspect relapse, but refuse to contact the treatment professionals or seek advice until there are overt problems on the job. By then, of course, the alcoholic is frequently causing major losses in productivity or endangering safety. So by the time intervention is undertaken, it may be too late to save the employee's position, or to protect the workplace from accident.

Therapists sometimes continue to treat alcoholics or addicts when they know drug use has resumed, in the hope that it will eventually stop. More often, it continues, with the therapist's inaction interpreted by the patient as tacit approval.

Another common mistake that therapists make is to attempt to *overcontrol* in an effort to prevent relapse—to pile direction on top of direction, assuming that more treatment is better treatment. Of course, that's not always true. And particularly in the case of relapse, the errors that are producing the relapse cycle are essentially simple, and, if they can be identified, may be remedied without undue stress.

Behavior-modification programs may actually become willing participants in the battle to regain control. Remember, it may not make sense to an alcoholic to submit to a difficult, expensive, often uncomfortable aversion or behavior-modification program only to completely *renounce* the drug. They may hope instead to regain a measure of control. And since behavioral psychologists traditionally regard alcoholism and drug dependency as behavior disorders rather than actual physiological diseases, they are in some respects only too eager to involve themselves in the search for control. The problem: if the program fails, it's the alcoholic who suffers, not the psychologist. He'll simply rationalize relapse in terms of a lack of patient motivation or a flaw in the conditioning program, and move on to the next case.

HOW TO AVOID THIS TRAP

It may sound odd, but the way to win this war is to surrender. Try the following exercise to help you understand the futility of this situation and to make changes in your approach.

Turn on your brain television. Remember, you have a volume control knob on the left which lets you modulate the intensity of anything you see on the screen: the brightness of the picture, the loudness of the sound. Right is up and left is down. You have a channel selector on the right side which lets you switch over to another show or to a blank screen or a test pattern if you want. Next to it is an on/off switch which you can reach at any time.

Now, let yourself relax. When you are ready, let a picture form on the screen.

It's an old Civil War movie. See the funny soldiers in their blue and gray uniforms. There's a battle raging. Soldiers are shooting one another, dropping like flies. The battlefield is littered with corpses. Yuck.

Let smoke fill the screen for a moment. You can't see anything; the smoke is so thick it's like a fog blanket. Then it starts to clear a little. You begin to see the outline of two soldiers, standing alone, at opposite ends of the screen.

One's in a blue uniform, the other in gray. That's about the only difference between them. They look like they might once have been handsome, but now they're skinny, battered-looking. It seems like the only thing that keeps them alive is the fact that they are at war with one another, and neither can stand the thought of the other one winning. Both raise their rifles and pull the trigger, but nothing happens. They're out of ammunition. Each pulls a pistol from his belt and tries to fire, but once again, nothing. They've used up all their weapons, and the only thing they have left is their fists.

They close, begin to fight. The gray soldier punches the blue in the mouth; the blue retaliates with a stiff right to the breadbasket. They wrestle briefly, then fall to the ground. The gray soldier is kneeling on top. He lands a good blow to the blue's face. The blue soldier manages to turn the gray over and straddles him. He too lands a blow to the face. The gray flips the blue soldier over and climbs atop him, once more landing a good blow. The blue struggles till he overturns the gray, gets to his knees and flails at his opponent. On and on they fight, exhausted but refusing to give up, rolling and punching, rolling and punching.

Now put yourself in the place of the gray soldier. Look at the blue through your eyes; he's on top and you're underneath. Watch it! There's a blow to your head. It hurts. Roll him over. You can do it; climb on top. Aha! Now he's yours, pinned beneath you. You raise your arm to strike him. Now pay attention: right before you strike—just as your arm begins its downward motion—you switch to the body of your victim.

Now you're the blue soldier. That bastard gray is on top, and his blow makes your head shiver. Summoning all your strength, you throw him off and climb to your knees. You prepare to retaliate. But hold on! You switch bodies again.

Now you're in the body of the gray soldier. Your enemy is getting ready to strike you, and try as you might, you can't avoid the blow . . . all you can do is throw him off and try to get in some damage of your own.

Wait a minute, you think. *There's something wrong here.* You never seem to feel any of your blows land on your enemy—never get the satisfaction of revenge. All you feel is your opponent making contact with your face! What kind of fight is this, where no matter how hard you struggle, you're always the loser? Where no matter who gets hit, you feel the pain?

Okay, that's enough. Reach forward and turn off the TV. Take a couple of breaths and let your eyes open.

That's what it's like to fight a war between the states. That's what it's like to go to war with a disease that makes its home in your own body. Trying to assert your will, and failing. How can you possibly win? Because every blow you strike lands on your own tender flesh. The harder you hit, the more damage you sustain.

Recognize that science has no cure for addiction. No way to restore your ability to use your drug without problems. To borrow an ancient example, it's a little like trying to change a pickle back into a cucumber: it's simply too late. The transformation only works one way.

To understand the myth of "just one," picture someone strapped in a chair. He's in some kind of a laboratory, and standing in front of him is a scientist. The scientist, dressed in a white lab coat, is pointing to a table with a variety of objects on it.

Look at the fellow in the chair. Wait a minute—it's you! You must have gone into a blackout and volunteered for some kind of weird experiment! And they've strapped you in this chair so you can't get out!

Look down at the table. There's quite an array: a beer, a glass of wine, and a mixed drink; a needle, a joint, and a pipe, obviously containing drugs; a plain cigarette (it's your brand) and a dish of your favorite food.

You turn your attention back to the scientist. He smiles.

"Welcome," he says, "to our experiment in self-control. Please select one of the substances on the table. Whichever you prefer—it's entirely up to you. Let me assure you that all are of the highest quality."

You look at the things on the table. Then you look back at the scientist.

"What's the rest of the experiment?" you ask.

"Oh, it's simple," he says. "You have the first one. That is to determine your preference. Then we continue to give you more of whatever you have selected, until you have consumed enough to make you violently ill."

"But what if I don't *want* so much?" you ask, quite certain that you won't.

"Oh, you see, that is the experiment. We know you will not want so much. That is our role: we will force you."

Now you're really confused. "But if you force me, that

doesn't say anything about my self-control. It just proves that you're stronger than I am."

"This is true."

"Then this whole thing doesn't make any sense."

The doctor shrugs. "Don't ask me. It's *your* experiment."

When you think about how good that first hit, first drink, first smoke, first cookie would taste, remember this: you don't really want *one* drink, *one* hit, *one* of anything. You want more. In fact, you want all the drinks, hits, smokes, and cookies in the known universe—up to and perhaps past the point where it threatens your life.

Cement this phrase into your brain: One is too many, and a thousand is not enough.

THREE EXERCISES TO REMIND YOURSELF THAT "JUST ONE" WON'T WORK

1. Make a sign (or have one made) that reads: *One is too many, and a thousand isn't enough.* Post it on the door of your refrigerator.
2. Have the above imprinted on your key ring. Read it every time you open a door.
3. Make a list of occasions in the past where you've set out to confine yourself to "just one" and failed. Describe each in some detail.

PROBLEMS OF BEING HUMAN

The second major obstacle in recovery is human nature. Whenever people want to make substantial changes in the way they live, they encounter three predictable traps.

First, you discover that your lifestyle may have developed a life of its own. Perhaps for the first time, you notice how things appear to have been arranged to *support* the very behavior you want to abandon. The world will seem to be full of cues and triggers that remind you of the way things used to be—and there are big holes in your routine where once you practiced the activity you've now eliminated. If you don't change this environment, it will lead you back where you left off.

A second obstacle has to do with stress. It's one thing to resolve to change when things are going smoothly. It's another thing to stick to your resolution when things get tough. If you can't deal with stress—or if you unwittingly hold on to attitudes that increase it—you're vulnerable to relapse at every crisis.

Third, human beings have an innate tendency toward complacency. Most of us look at problems as though we were lining up for a hundred-yard dash: we want to go all out, win the race, celebrate victory, and rest on our laurels. Addiction, however, is a marathon. We have to learn to pace ourselves, to be vigilant against relapse, to guard against overconfidence.

It's these three problems that form the core of traps four, five, and six. Read on.

THE FOURTH TRAP: MAINTAINING A HIGH-RISK LIFESTYLE

"It's like one day you realize that you don't fit in with the dope people anymore. But you don't fit in with the straight people, either. So where the hell do you fit?"

—Recovering addict, age 19

Recovery means more than simply giving up alcohol and drugs. It also means abandoning key aspects of the lifestyle associated with them. For some people, that is the bigger sacrifice.

The addictive lifestyle doesn't spring up by accident. Addiction requires that you build your life around drug use. It becomes the centerpiece of daily existence—the fulcrum around which everything else revolves.

The life of an addict is organized around a different set of goals than that of a nonaddict. Where normal people base their activities on the need to eat and rest and relate to others, your life as an addict must be dominated by the provision and maintenance of a drug supply. You devote the same kind of care and attention to obtaining and using drugs as nonaddicts do to eating, loving, and work. More, perhaps.

It's a lifestyle that obviously requires a certain degree of secrecy, manipulation, and outright lying. Admittedly, nonaddicts are easy to deceive. If you don't know what to look for, the telltale signs of addiction can be almost invisible. That's why so many otherwise intelligent parents and teachers and friends and employers remain blissfully unaware while drug use goes on all around them. Once you do know the signs, you'll be amazed at how much goes on right under your nose.

It's less apparent but no less real for those who become addicted to alcohol. One of the central requirements for inclusion in an alcoholic's social circle is that you drink as much as or more than he does. Where the nonalcoholic selects his friends on the basis of similar interests, compatible hobbies, et cetera, the alcoholic often picks associates on the basis of the amount and frequency of their drinking.

In the same vein, alcoholics surround themselves with *enablers:* people who unwittingly protect them from the consequences of their own drinking. For example, we have an alcoholic physician as a patient who deteriorated mentally to the point where he was writing notes in the wrong chart, making obviously incorrect diagnoses. For years, this escalating deterioration was masked by his secretary (who handled all the office business, remembered deadlines, cleaned up administrative messes he left behind) and his office nurse (who made sure nobody died from his errors). The other physician in the practice, who also happens to be his best friend, was profoundly stunned to learn that his partner had liver cirrhosis. "I didn't even know he drank," the doctor exclaimed.

The point: this is his peer group. This is the tight circle of associates to whom he will return following treatment. And each and every one of these individuals has demonstrated a profound inability to recognize and deal with alcoholism.

So your circle of friends may actually reinforce and perpetuate the addictive cycle. This makes it easier to remain in denial, to "compare out" with others. You can insist with considerable justification that you aren't that much different from anybody else you know—which is more a reflection on the company you keep than on the presence or absence of addiction.

Eventually, you bottom out. Loss of control overcomes even the ability of other alcoholics to ignore it. By the time you finally arrive in treatment, just about everyone you know is part of this subculture. These folks—not the nonalcoholics of the world—are your "extended family." And sometimes you have trouble giving them up.

There's a second factor. Many alcoholics and drug addicts in treatment remain dependent on people or environments that probably aren't conducive to staying sober. You may have shared drugs with people at work. Adolescents often return to the place where they got turned on to drugs in the first place: high school. More than a few alcoholics work in bars and restaurants where drinking is the norm, not the exception. And it isn't uncommon for a counselor to discover that the person coming to family sessions in order to help the addict also has a drug or alcohol problem. It runs in families.

Imagine you've only recently detoxified from drugs or alcohol. You know there's something about the way you live that you probably ought to change, if you intend to stay sober. But you know intuitively that change has a price. There's a *risk* associated with it. And you realize that as much as you need to, you simply don't want to take this risk and pay this price at this point in your life.

So perhaps you decide not to try. Instead, you convince yourself that through strength of conviction or single-mindedness of purpose, you're going to be able to continue living as you have been, with one exception: you're no longer using booze or drugs.

Of course, you may know someone who's already done this. If so, you'll point to them as evidence that you, too, will ultimately succeed.

Thus you fall headlong into the trap. Setting out to be an island of sobriety in a sea of drunkenness, you convince yourself that you are temptation-proof. That superior willpower, intelligence, education, determination, or plain luck will permit you to succeed where others have failed.

Most of the time, it doesn't.

ATTITUDE CHECK #4: HIGH-RISK ENVIRONMENT

To find out the extent to which your lifestyle qualifies as high-risk answer yes or no to the following statements. If you have any questions, discuss them with a counselor or sponsor before answering.

1. Most of my friends drink or use drugs.
2. Many of my friends drink or use drugs as much or more than I do.
3. Before entering treatment, I drank or used drugs more days than I did not.
4. Most of the social occasions I have attended in the last two years have included alcohol or drugs.
5. I have very few recovering friends.
6. I think I will feel awkward at social occasions where other people drink if I do not.
7. I am concerned about making new friends who are drug- and alcohol-free.
8. I am concerned about running into friends and associates from the past.
9. I think it would be difficult for me to stay sober or clean if I were to hang around people who used alcohol and drugs.

10. I wonder what I will do with my time now that I am not using alcohol or drugs.
11. I wonder how I will socialize with people now that I'm not using alcohol or drugs.
12. I still experience periodic cravings for alcohol or drugs.

Look at the box that follows for an interpretation of the results.

If you answered "yes" to one or two of the questions your chance of relapse is low. If you answered "yes" to three or four of the questions your chance of relapse is moderate and you should continue to learn and be aware of the pitfalls of recovery. If you answered "yes" to five or six of the questions you are at high risk for relapse and should pay particular attention to this trap. If you answered "yes" to seven or more of the questions you are in a relapse "red zone" and need to seek and follow good advice immediately.

HOW THE TRAP CLOSES

Sometimes you recognize danger to your sobriety but convince yourself that you *must,* by virtue of some overriding concern, remain in a high-risk situation. Here's how most people go about it, and what happens as a result.

The underlying assumption: That you can stay sober in a slippery environment. Normally, you justify staying in this environment by insisting that "circumstances" make it impossible to change, at least temporarily.

Resulting behavior: You set up a situation in which you pit your strength against the disease in an environment that doesn't support sobriety.

The second decision: Confronted with ongoing temptation, you attempt to take your mind off it by focussing on other problems. You may become so preoccupied with your struggle to control the high-risk situation that you forget about mundane issues such as staying off alcohol and drugs. Frequently the object of this preoccupation (or in some cases, obsession) is *someone else's* behavior (especially drinking or drug use).

Resulting behavior: You lose sight of your own recovery.

The third decision: You take the position of relying on personal willpower to remain sober.

Resulting behavior: You further isolate yourself from recovery-oriented support groups. At some point, a crisis arises—a severe craving, an argument, a dilemma at work or home—and there is no one around to help.

The fourth decision: You decide to have "one" drink or drug, just to get through this particular situation.

Resulting behavior: Relapse.

RED FLAGS

1. "Damn it, I just know I can get through this on my own . . . if I have enough cooperation from other people."
2. "I know a guy who stayed sober even while he was working as a bartender. And I met a woman in AA whose husband is still drinking and smoking marijuana. So don't tell me it isn't possible. I've seen it."
3. "I really don't have any choice in the matter. I don't have anywhere else to go (to live, to work, to associate, et cetera).

I just can't disassociate myself from drugs completely. Do you expect me to live in an ivory tower somewhere?"

4. "I know I should make a change, but this situation is only temporary . . . I'll make a move as soon as I can (afford it, find the right location, meet the right people, complete a goal, et cetera)."

5. "You can't expect me to change everything at once. I can only handle so much at a time."

RELAPSE IN ACTION

Owen B. and the Girl of His Dreams

Let's let Owen B. tell his own story:

I can't remember exactly when I first decided that I wanted to quit drinking and doing drugs. I'd been in it since I was a kid—long enough that I found myself unable to recall what I was like before I started filling my brain cells with assorted substances. Once I discovered my talent for guitar and my ambitions in rock and roll, I guess my fate was just about sealed. I'd use drugs until I died. And I think if it wasn't for Jenny, I'd have done just that.

Jenny was my wife, my best friend, and my dope partner. If you believe a junkie can love another human being as much as he loves dope, that's how I felt about Jenny. Her overdose—and my all-night vigil at the hospital, worrying that she wasn't going to make it—was what drove me into the treatment center. I made a vow that night that things were going to get better, and that she and I would have a chance at the straight life, no matter what it took.

Jenny came to visit me every weekend while I was in the hospital getting straight. She didn't look very good herself, but

I chalked that up to the aftereffects of her OD, you know? Plus she had never been very healthy. Two weeks before I was to be released, we signed a contract on a house. It was a big deal for me—like a symbol that I was growing up, at last.

Anyway, we moved in, and for the next month or so I did pretty well. I went to the gym every day and worked out, and swam laps in my pool every evening, and was careful about what I ate. All in all, I was pretty pleased with myself. I hadn't gotten up the nerve to see any of the guys in the band—I knew they were still heavily into dope.

Then it happened. I was going through the bank statement one day—another of those simple duties I'd never in a million years dreamed I would ever do—and I noticed a bunch of cash withdrawals from the automatic teller. At first, I didn't think anything of it. But later, I went back through the previous months' statements, and it was pretty clear—either somebody had my bank card, or Jenny was pulling about a thousand bucks a month extra out of our account. Over and above what I could see her spending. And as much as I tried to deny it, I knew exactly what that money was going for.

I figured that if I confronted her, she'd just blow her top or lie to me. I decided to follow her the next day, when she went out to the store. And sure enough, she made a detour, to a crummy motel on Dolores where she could cop. I sat in the car wishing I was some straight husband who had just found out his wife was having an affair. But I knew Jenny wasn't looking for a boyfriend.

I waited till she left, then followed her home. When I walked in, she was all hyper. I said nothing, just slapped her and pushed her onto the couch. She was yelling and kicking like a madwoman. I got her skirt up and checked her thigh for tracks. I couldn't believe I hadn't noticed them before.

She told me she was copping from a small-time pimp

named Reggie Jones who I knew. I went out looking for him. I had a ferocious headache, the kind that feels like somebody's driving nails into your skull. I took along a Saturday night special that I'd picked up back when I was using, just in case somebody tried to rip me off. I came up with what I thought was a pretty good plan. Phase one: I was going to blow Reggie Jones's ugly head right off his shoulders. Phase two: I was going to do the same to myself.

I got to his crib about three in the afternoon. Reggie met me at the door in one of those three-hundred-dollar silk bathrobes. I kept the gun in my pocket, and asked him to step outside for a minute, so we could talk.

"Reggie," I told him, struggling to keep my voice steady, "have you been messing with my wife?" He shook his head no. But he was lying, and I knew it.

I pulled the gun out and held it to his cheek. I thought he was going to cry.

"Question two," I said. "Have you gotten her strung out again?"

He shook his head. "She was already strung out when she come to me. She ain't never stopped."

"You lying piece of shit," I said. But he wasn't, of course. There was the missing piece: Jenny hadn't been clean and fallen off the wagon. She'd been dirty the entire time.

He hadn't used her. She'd used Reggie. And I was the chump.

I brought the gun down, relaxing the hammer as I did. All of a sudden, I was very, very tired. Like there wasn't any more purpose in my doing anything, except maybe laying down and dying. Because when you stopped to think, what did any of this shit matter? And who was I, thinking I was hot stuff because I wasn't sticking a needle in my arm, because I was trotting off every night to sit with a bunch of pious churchies and look down on everybody else in the real world? There wasn't one thing in the whole world I could think of that was honestly worth the energy it took to do it.

Well, maybe I could think of *one* thing.

I smiled at Reggie. "Sorry, man," I said. "Got a little hot there for a minute. No hard feelings, huh?" I gave him a big grin. "Say, bro, you got any dope?"

Reggie just looked at me. I could tell he thought I was crazy as a shithouse rat. But he also believed me.

I threw an arm around his shoulders, and we went inside.

Discussion: Owen B.

Owen denies, rationalizes, externalizes, and minimizes his drug use, until he finally comes to realize that there are some events—the near death of the woman he loves—that he simply cannot excuse. But once sober, he simply switches the object of his defensiveness from heroin to Jenny. In the first place, he never doubts that she, too, has given up drugs—though any heroin addict will tell you the chances of that without help are slim. It seems curious that Jenny's near-death affected him much more than it did her (until you realize that she slept through the overdose). Thus Owen "hit bottom"—became motivated to change—while she didn't.

Second, he unquestioningly accepts her excuses for not attending Narcotics Anonymous or any other recovery program. Someone with her history needs all the help she can get. If she can't involve herself in NA, she'd better find *something* to lean on.

And when the signs of relapse do begin to appear, he simply ignores them. Sure, we can all understand this—who wants to see someone you love falling by the wayside?—but the practical effect is to leave Owen in a state of denial. That in turn makes him extraordinarily vulnerable to the kind of crushing blow he receives as he realizes that his version of reality is collapsing around him. That the woman he wants so badly to succeed has in fact hardly even made an attempt.

Yes, she's been lying to him. But nowhere near as much as he's been lying to himself.

CO-DEPENDENT ROLE IN THIS TRAP

It's ironic how often the recovering alcoholic or addict finds himself playing enabler to someone else, thus ensuring at least one relationship with a "slippery person." Owen becomes co-dependent to his wife's addictive behavior, making the same errors that other people made when they were trying to get him to stop taking drugs. Like other co-dependents, he finds his attention focused on her to the point of obsession. And that of course precludes paying heed to his own fragile sobriety.

HOW TO AVOID THIS TRAP

First, let's identify potential slippery places and people in your life in the past.

Turn on your brain TV. On the screen you see another episode of *This Is Your Life*. It's a rerun. You're at the worst point of your addiction—when you were drinking the most, using the most, whatever. Now, watch yourself going through the motions of a typical day. Get up in the morning. Brush your teeth. Go to work. All the stuff you normally do. Take particular note of any *people* who are around when you drink or get high, or any particular *environment* that you associate with that process. If you feel a craving coming on, simply reach forward to the "volume" dial and turn it down so that it doesn't bother you. Remember, a craving is utterly harmless.

If you notice that there are perhaps one or two people or one or two places that are almost always involved in your drug use, pay particular attention to them. For example, if there's a friend or lover who keeps showing up on your TV show whenever you start to drink or use, take special note. Same thing with special places or situations that are usually associated with drug use. Remember them. Make a list in your mind—write it out on a piece of mental paper—and draw a little flag next to each one. Those are danger flags, by the way. You want to avoid these in the future.

Same goes for people or situations that directly encourage a desire to drink or use drugs—even if the people themselves are drug-free. For example, there might be someone you always argue with, so that just being around them is usually enough to get you thinking about getting high. Or maybe there's a person toward whom you hold a particularly strong resentment, so that every time you think about them, you find yourself getting angrier and angrier. Once again, use the volume knob to control the intensity of these feelings. It's not that different from controlling a craving. Just reach forward and turn the knob to low if you like.

Done? Now, reach forward and change the channel so that the screen is blank. Nothing on it.

Okay, let's start a new episode, which is different from the first. You're still the star, but now it's your life *at the present moment.* And instead of watching a repeat episode of an old show, we're going to write one as we go. Start by repeating the basic plot: a day in the life of You. Get up in the morning, brush your teeth, go to work. There is no drinking or drug use at all. Just keep watching. See any slippery places or situations in there? In particular, notice any cravings coming up? If you do, remember you can control them with the volume knob. Just turn it down.

Once again, pull out your list of "slipperies." Are there any people in your new TV show who

1. may have alcohol or drug problems themselves?
2. have done drugs with you in the past?

3. have provided excuses for drinking or drug use, by arguing, withholding affection, et cetera?

Write down any new entries that weren't on your original list. Flag them as before.

When you're finished, turn off the TV. Open your eyes. Now take the list that's in your head and put it down on paper. After each name of a person or a situation, put a short explanation of (1) the role this plays in your life (such as "my boyfriend" or "where I go to work,") and (2) how important it is to maintain this contact even though you're sober. In other words, are you going to continue to expose yourself to slippery places and people? If so, why? What is your reasoning?

Now take this list to a counselor or sponsor or other knowledgeable person, and go over it with them. How do they feel about your list? Do they agree with your assessment?

Finished? Then figure out how to do the following:

1. eliminate slippery people and places from your life
2. where you can't, how you're going to avoid relapsing until you can

Now go over this with the counselor or sponsor. Get their feedback. Do they think you have a good plan? Ask them where they think you are still vulnerable.

Using this feedback, revise your plan.

Now wait one day. Then turn on the brain TV once more, and start the tape of your everyday life. Play out the situations you have identified as likely to occur in the future, and try out your solutions. Do they work? How well? Try out other situations until it seems to you that you are handling them fairly well and you are able to modulate your own emotions somewhat.

Do the final exercise once weekly for the first twenty weeks of recovery.

SOME ANSWERS TO COMMON QUESTIONS ABOUT A HIGH-RISK LIFESTYLE

1. Most of my friends drink or use drugs.

Not surprising, is it? If they didn't, you probably would have avoided them during your active drinking. That's one of the roles that AA and NA play in the lives of recovering people: they offer an opportunity to make friends who are not only sober but understand what addiction is all about.

2. Many of my friends drink or use drugs as much as or more than I do. What does this say about my own problem?

Again, it's probably more a reflection on your choice of friends than on whether or not you have alcoholism or drug addiction.

3. What do I do at social occasions where alcohol is served? About invitations to parties?

There's a terrific little book called *Living Sober* (AA World Services), which addresses questions like this. You can probably buy it at an AA meeting or through your local Intergroup.

4. How do I make new friends who are drug- and alcohol-free?

Start by introducing yourself at Twelve Step meetings. Get a sponsor, if only a temporary one. If you hear someone say something you like at a meeting, be sure to introduce yourself. If there's one in your area, join an AA or NA club. Go to the social affairs.

THE FIFTH TRAP:
STRESS

"It seems like no matter what I do, something always goes wrong. Am I being punished or something?"

—Recovering Addict

Everyone experiences stress. There's no escape. From the moment of birth to the day we die, our lives are filled with problems large and small. No matter how we try, we never solve them all.

That's the human condition. Still, some of us handle it better than others.

Of course, recovery from addictive disease adds an extra dimension to the problem. In the first place, you're making some fairly profound changes in the way you live. This in itself is stressful. At the same time, your brain is struggling to adjust to life without the chemical support upon which it has become dependent. Remember: on a cellular level, the brain can't fathom your decision to give up alcohol and drugs. *We* need *them,* the nerve cells cry out. Brain cells are not impressed by the argument that continued use would result in death. *That's* your *problem,* they seem to say.

As time passes, the brain recalls the days when it functioned without the aid of drugs, and abandons its demand for foreign substances. But this doesn't happen overnight. While it's taking place, you're especially vulnerable to overreactions of all types—including a dangerously exaggerated response to normal stress. That's why we identify and address habits and attitudes that might inadvertently promote stress.

THE ROLE OF STRESS IN EVERYDAY LIFE

Try thinking of stress as a physiological rather than a psychological phenomenon. The brain is charged with regulating your response to the environment so as to maintain *homeostasis* (stability within the organism). To accomplish this, the brain includes a number of regulating mechanisms. Step outside on a cold day or climb into a hot bath: the brain immediately adjusts your body temperature to accommodate your changed conditions and preserve the body's integrity. Take a drug for a cold or headache or simply to get high, and the brain responds with the appropriate alterations in its own chemistry. There's no volition involved; it occurs below the level of consciousness. As far as you're concerned, it's automatic.

The brain's approach to danger in the larger environment—from an enemy, for example—centers around the fight-or-flight response: a sudden rush of hormones that both motivates and supports self-defense. Your pulse speeds up. Your attention focuses entirely on the perceived threat. When you're experiencing fight-or-flight, you can't eat, sleep, or concentrate on anything but avoiding danger. If you can run, you will; if not, you'll turn and fight. The brain won't permit you to relax until you've done one or the other, or the danger has passed.

It's enormously effective, as the survival of humanity in a hostile world would suggest. Yet there are some inherent flaws in this mechanism. In the first place, the brain must rely on its perceptions to identify a threat. If these perceptions are inaccurate—or if they are incorrectly interpreted—you could become a victim of your own fight-or-flight response. You might find yourself reacting to dangers that don't really exist.

Remember: though fear itself is hard-wired into the brain, you learn to identify danger largely through experience. The brain learns what to fear in much the same way you learn to ride a bicycle. Once learned, it's never entirely forgotten.

There are two key differences between the stress you experience and that suffered by your neighbor. First, your nervous system may be jangling a bit louder than his, at least for a while. And second, you don't have the luxury of turning to alcohol or drugs to soothe it.

From the standpoint of the recovering person, stress is the ultimate distraction. When your brain is preoccupied with fight-or-flight, it's impossible to concentrate on mundane concerns such as staying sober. That's what makes this trap so dangerous. And that's why every recovering alcoholic must devote considerable attention to learning to deal with stress.

ATTITUDE CHECK #5: STRESS PROFILE

Let's see what kind of problems vex you the most. Answer yes or no to the following statements.

1. If you want something done right, you'd better do it yourself.
2. I hate having to wait for something.
3. I'm a worrier.
4. I often feel as though other people are taking advantage of me.
5. I think people are basically just looking out for themselves.
6. Nothing irritates me like incompetence.
7. If I'm doing something well, I want to be rewarded right away.
8. When I have something on my mind, I often have a hard time sleeping or concentrating.
9. I feel I have to put up with a lot from other people.
10. I'm slow to trust people.
11. I like everything to be in its place.
12. If I want something, I want it *now*.

13. If something isn't right in my life, I can't get anything else done until it's resolved.
14. I often find myself in conflict with other people.
15. I tend to be suspicious of other peoples' motives.
16. I often feel as though I'm not getting enough accomplished.
17. I am easily discouraged when I can't solve a problem.
18. I don't understand what people are talking about when they tell me to "stop worrying" about something.
19. I think my life has been a lot harder than most.
20. I find it very hard to open up to people.
21. I feel that most people don't expect enough from themselves.
22. Little things irritate me more than big difficulties.
23. Sometimes I dread getting up in the morning and facing the new day.
24. If people understood my problems, they'd be more sympathetic.
25. I think if someone takes advantage of you, it's your own fault for trusting them.

Look at the box below for an interpretation of the results.

If you answered "yes" to five or less of the questions your chance of relapse is low. If you answered "yes" to between six and fifteen of the questions your chance of relapse is moderate and you should continue to learn and be aware of the pitfalls of recovery. If you answered "yes" to between sixteen and twenty of the questions you are at high risk for relapse and should pay particular attention to this trap. If you answered "yes" to 20 or more of the questions you are in a relapse "red zone" and need to seek and follow good advice immediately.

HOW THE TRAP CLOSES

The stress trap is based on certain underlying assumptions that you make about recovery and, in fact, about life in general. They are:

That there exist certain situations which cannot be tolerated yet cannot be changed.

That such situations necessitate some kind of temporary "escape."

That alcohol and drugs are the most effective way to escape.

That the need for a temporary relief from stress justifies using alcohol and drugs, no matter what the consequences.

Here's how these assumptions are translated into a relapse.

The first decision: You decide you have a problem that can't be corrected or endured.

Resulting behavior: Begins cycle of worry and obsessive thinking.

The second decision: Escalating stress causes strong desire for temporary relief.

Resulting behavior: Looks for methods to relieve symptoms rather than address problem.

The third decision: Other concerns fade into background as *stress* becomes predominant problem and focus of attention.

Resulting behavior: Symptoms of stress proliferate (insomnia, anxiety, irritability, et cetera).

The fourth decision: You begin to question if sobriety is worth the effort.

Resulting behavior: Euphoric memory of drug effect; forget bad parts of drug experience.

The fifth decision: You decide to obtain relief, regardless of the consequences.

Resulting behavior: Reintroduce drug, perhaps following a crisis that "justifies" giving up.

As you allow worry to escalate to obsessive proportions, you may seek advice, but will then reject it in favor of continuing along the same path.

RED FLAGS

You know you're near this trap because phrases like the following begin to creep into your thinking or conversation:

1. "People tell me not to dwell on my problems, but I just can't help it."
2. "You don't understand. If you had my problems, you'd react the same way."
3. "It's just too awful to bear."
4. "I can't take the time out for other things until I get this resolved."
5. "It's really starting to get to me . . . I lie awake at night worrying . . ."
6. "Sometimes I think, God, a drink (smoke, hit) would feel really good right about now . . ."
7. "If I'd known sobriety was going to be like this, I'd never have even tried."
8. "I'll do the best I can, but I'm not promising if things get worse I won't slip."
9. "I feel worse now than when I was drinking."

STRESS AS A PROBLEM IN LIVING

There are two things to keep in mind when talking about how stress impacts your life.

Rule One: Different people respond differently to different forms of stress.

In other words, the greatest variable in stress is *who* happens to be experiencing it. The most common illustration is a simple airplane flight. The range of tension and anxiety among the hundred and fifty persons on board is remarkable. And remember, there are a whole lot of people who were too nervous even to get on that plane in the first place!

Some people have a profound fear of being unemployed or out of money. Others cheerfully take financial risks that would precipitate a heart attack in their more security-conscious brethren.

All of us have certain activities we find more stressful than others. We know one psychologist who absolutely cannot tolerate being late to anything, even when it's caused by events beyond his control. He frets and fumes until he's unable to deliver the speech he's flown 1,500 miles to give. Still another friend has no tolerance for any type of physical illness. A sprained ankle sends her right to bed. You can imagine what happens every time her back goes out. Her friends dread the day.

Not to belabor the point: The things that drive one person insane often aren't nearly as damaging to someone sitting right across the aisle on Flight 291. It's all relative.

Rule Two: You can learn to manage stress differently than you have in the past.

This is another one of those things that most people know and yet they don't. By that we mean that if you took a poll, most respondents would agree with the above statement, but if you set up a hidden camera and observed them for forty-eight hours, you'd see that they act as though their reactions to stress are set in concrete and there's absolutely nothing they can do about it.

There's a real gap between what people believe about stress

and what they actually do when they find themselves in a stressful situation. Intellectually, most of us believe that stress can be controlled. On a deeper level, we act as if it can't.

Cognitive psychologists teach us that a stress reaction can be divided into its component parts. First, there's the event itself. Second, there's your *interpretation* of the event. Third, there's your *emotional reaction.* The second and third component combine to produce the fourth, which is your *response* to the event. This in turn often influences future events, and may in fact contribute directly to further stress.

This is the model we used in Chapter 4. It can be diagrammed as follows:

Event   →   *Interpretation*   →   *Feeling*   →   *Response*

Therapists strive to teach people to reduce stress by addressing it in terms of these components. A biofeedback program might teach you to slow your pulse by training yourself to recognize certain cues that let you know you're getting too excited. An expressive therapist would instruct you to get in touch with certain *feelings* in hopes of reducing their intensity through a process of emotional resolution. A cognitive therapist would strive to change your *interpretation* of what happened, knowing that in most cases, it's the interpretation that's making you upset, rather than the event itself.

The average person, on the other hand, takes a different approach. We delude ourselves that we can change the event itself.

Suppose you have an argument with someone. Do you ever find yourself replaying the conversation over and over again in your head? Only this time you're saying lots of clever things you never said in the original discussion? (So we're not the only people in the world who do this!)

What's the purpose? Simply to make things turn out the way you think they should have in the first place. When you replay the conflict, you let yourself win. It's a little game we play with ourselves.

Another way to impose your personal vision on the universe is to cling emotionally to long-dead events. If somebody yells at you when you're a little kid and you never forgive them for it, then you're keeping your relationship fixed at that one point in time. You're acting as if the only way to deal with your feelings is to change the event that offended you in the first place. But as you well know, that can never be changed. To do so, you would have to challenge time itself.

Imagine for a moment that time is an enormous river and that you're floating along in a rather feeble-looking boat. You pass a particularly nice looking section of riverbank and ten minutes later decide that you'd like to go back and explore that area in depth. But when you try to paddle back, you discover that the river has an enormously strong current that makes it impossible. You want to return to where you were, but the river won't let you. It simply doesn't flow that way. And you've got no choice but to go where it does.

Aha! you think, *I'll drop an anchor.* But you discover that the anchor won't hold. Your boat hesitates for a few minutes, then pulls loose and is on its way again—this time trailing an anchor. Pretty soon, your little boat has a dozen or so of these useless things lagging along behind it. They're not enough to bring you to a stop. They just slow you down.

That's what it's like when you try to alter an event that has already happened: it's an exercise in futility. On the other hand, you may be able to alter your original *interpretation*—your idea of its meaning. That could conceivably make you feel a lot better. And you *can* change it, because it's been floating down the river along with you.

Back to stress: because people act as if they can't really change the way they respond to problems, it's easy for them to make the next leap toward the idea that they need to escape from reality. That there is no other option. And since "escaping reality" is synonymous in the mind of the addict with using alcohol or drugs, it's a major precipitant of relapse.

Now, here's an example.

RELAPSE IN ACTION

The Grapevine

Bobby Lee Paine suffered the embarrassment of getting caught on a routine drug screen at a football training camp. Bobby's humiliation was made even worse by the fact that at the end of the previous season, his teammates had voted him cocaptain. The test was positive for marijuana, but Bobby's wife told the doctor that Bobby was a cocaine user and the team insisted he go through a rehabilitation program. He did, and found that he felt a great deal better drug-free. So he made a little vow to himself: he would follow the program and renounce all drugs, at least during playing season.

Coincidentally, Bobby had also completed his option year and was in effect playing without a contract. At first, he and his agent Max thought the negotiations would be fairly simple; Bobby had been a Pro Bowl alternate the previous year, and they both expected a substantial raise.

But Bobby Lee wasn't prepared for the new general manager. During their first negotiating session, the general manager referred to Bobby as an "aging" linebacker, with "limited" prospects for the future, "arthritic knees," "waning" coverage skills, and "personal problems." Bobby couldn't understand how the same fellow could then turn around and tell the newspapers how much they wanted Bobby Lee to stay with the team and help them to the championship. It just didn't make sense. Max explained to Bobby Lee that the GM was just trying to make Bobby look bad to lower his eventual price. But Bobby

Lee took this to heart. Though they eventually agreed on a generous contract, Bobby Lee wasn't able to put the experience out of his mind. It soured him on the team and the sport, and even though the team continued winning, he didn't seem to enjoy it. He began to argue with his wife and even had some trouble sleeping before games. He kept wondering if the team was going to trade him to a losing team or some franchise nobody wanted to go to. He stopped talking to his counselor, using the excuse that his training schedule didn't permit it, but really because he couldn't stand to talk about this issue anymore. "It's taking my mind off the game," he told Max. "I've just got to stop thinking about it." But the more he tried not to think about it, the more he found himself thinking about it.

Bobby became depressed. He stopped talking to most of his teammates and fell into a pattern in which he would show up at the park, sleep through team meetings, and in general just go through the motions. Shortly before the playoffs, a sportswriter told Bobby Lee that the GM was shopping him around the league as a middle-round draft choice. Bobby Lee exploded, shoved the reporter out of the way, and stormed into the office of the head coach. After twenty minutes of screaming at each other, Bobby Lee picked up a trophy off the coach's desk and hurled it through a window. The coach immediately suspended him without pay and declared him finished for the season. Bobby Lee stormed out of the coach's office and went home.

Later that night, Bobby Lee cooled down enough to realize what he had done—jeopardized a $500,000-per-year job, because of a rumor. He sat on the edge of the bed, thinking, *I've really screwed it up now . . .*

After an hour or so, he dug out his address book and found a phone number. Three days later, his wife and the police found him, unconscious, in a cheap hotel room. There was a crack pipe in his hand and several empty fifths of Puerto Rican rum on the bed beside him.

Note how as the story progresses, Bobby becomes his own worst enemy. He obsesses over the general manager's remarks, refuses to be reassured by his agent, lets his resentment destroy even his pleasure in winning. It's as though he enters into a conspiracy to get himself suspended. That's characteristic of this trap. You perceive stress as outside yourself and therefore beyond your control—when in reality, your discomfort springs from your own thinking.

CO-DEPENDENT ROLE IN THIS TRAP

The Problem Junkie and the Human Pain Reliever

Perhaps as much as any, this particular relapse trap depends on the involvement of other people. Because its victims normally experience an extended period of escalating problems, they often cultivate one or more confidants with whom to discuss worries, vent feelings, obtain sympathy and advice, which seems to provide temporary relief. We call such people (often co-dependents themselves) *pain relievers.* In some cases, the type of attention provided by a human pain reliever becomes an end in itself. Relapse, and the stress that excuses it, forms the basis for a new type of relationship, based on asking for and receiving an almost continual stream of emotional succor. In turn, the "helper," or advice-giver, may be attracted by the sheer weight of the relapser's overt need. This conveniently meshes with the co-dependent's "need to be needed." A symbiosis develops in which the relapser is constantly seeking help for an array of difficulties and the pain reliever is constantly striving to provide better and better solutions. Each must continually shove to the back of his or her consciousness the fact that the relapser shows little improvement, and in fact may be worsening.

When someone is caught in a vortex of problems, every

more-than-superficial relationship turns into a cross between psychotherapy and "Dear Abby." Thus the relapser may unconsciously maintain a considerable level of chronic stress as a means of justifying his or her need for almost constant support. When this happens, we say he or she has become a "stress addict" or "problem junkie." Problem junkies nurture problems like oysters nurture pearls; though guidance may be actively sought, real solutions are overtly rejected or at least never implemented. That's because life without problems is inconceivable. Chaos has become "normal," and the "helping relationship" is the only kind that can be sustained.

The enabler in this relapse trap can be a professional helper—a counselor, therapist, or physician—or sometimes an AA sponsor, close friend, concerned parent, or family member. Here's an example of such a relationship in action. Marina, an inveterate stress addict and chronic relapser, is complaining about her relationship with her boyfriend to Rhonda, her sponsor.

MARINA: I just don't know what to do. Sometimes I want to kill him. I mean it. Last night I had a dream I had stabbed him . . . it was so real, I woke up covered with sweat from head to toe. And you know what? When I realized it was a dream, I was disappointed. I know I would have gone to jail, but it would have been worth it to see him get what he deserves.

RHONDA: Now, now, honey, you're letting him get to you again. Remember, he can't hurt you if you don't let him. That's why you have to stop getting all upset and drinking when he disappears the way he does.

MARINA: I know you're right, but I can't stand it when he does that.

RHONDA: Why don't you move in with your friend Barbara?

MARINA: You know I can't stand to live with somebody else. I'm just not built that way.

RHONDA: But he's abusing you, both emotionally and physically . . .

MARINA: But I just can't up and leave. I still love him. I know you must think I'm crazy, but I do. I want to kill him, but I love him. I must be crazy, right?

RHONDA: No, no, don't say that. But if you're going to stay with him, you'll have to learn not to have these arguments. How to avoid provoking him.

MARINA: That's not right. Why should I do all the adjusting? He's the one who's abusing me. Why should I be the one to hide every time he comes home drunk and wants to make love to me . . . I'm not going to put up with that. I'm not.

Rhonda and Marina have a push-me–pull-you relationship, not unlike the one Marina has with Freddy. Whenever Rhonda offers a suggestion, Marina counters with an obstacle—not insurmountable, but enough to make Rhonda strive for a better, more perfect solution. The problem junkie must keep the pain reliever on the line, offering suggestions, sympathy, warmth, and support—which are the problem junkie's real goals in the relationship. The pain reliever, on the other hand, must convince herself that the problem junkie is actually seeking a solution. But that solution, remember, would mean a change in and perhaps an end to the relationship with the co-dependent, and the relapser does not want that.

The solution? Most "pain relievers" eventually realize the futility of their task and break off the relationship, often at considerable emotional cost to both parties. The extraordinary level of dependence that develops may lead the co-dependent to worry about a suicide attempt on the part of the relapser. An alternate solution for the pain reliever: change the *role* you play in the problem junkie's life.

HOW TO AVOID THIS TRAP

There are five common sources of chronic stress for the recovering person. The first is the habit of *perfectionism*. The second is a low tolerance for *frustration*. The third involves obsessive *worrying*. Fourth is a backlog of *resentments* from the past. Number five centers around a basic *mistrust* of others. These can combine to create and sustain an unacceptable level of stress in your life.

Let's start by categorizing the things you find stressful.

Exercise One:

Go back to the stress profile on pages 133–34. This time, we'll add the scores differently.

Count your positive responses to statements 1, 6, 11, 16, and 21 only. Write this number in the margin. This is your total for the *Perfectionism* scale—your tendency to expect too much from yourself and others.

Next, count your positive responses to statements 2, 7, 12, 17, and 22. Write this number in the margin. This is your total for the *Frustration Tolerance* scale—your ability to handle delays, postponements, and unforeseen obstacles.

Count your positive responses to statements 3, 8, 13, 18, and 23 only. This is your total for the *Obsessive* scale—your tendency to dwell on problems to the point where it interferes with your other activities.

Then, count your positive responses to statements 4, 9, 14, 19, and 24. This is your total for the *Resentment* scale—your feeling of having been victimized, prejudiced against, or taken advantage of by others.

Last, count your positive responses to statements 5, 10, 15,

20, and 25 only. This is your total for the *Mistrust* scale—your tendency to expect the worst from other people.

Wherever you answered "yes" to more than three statements in any category, be sure to read the ensuing explanation and complete the suggested exercises (below). Pay special attention to the two highest scores—those are the areas where stress is most likely to appear.

Category A: Perfectionism

Perfectionism is the habit of demanding an unrealistic level of performance. The perfectionist imposes his own standards and values on other people, which inevitably creates conflict. Even when he gets his way, he's unhappy—after all, a perfectionist by definition is never satisfied. Perfectionists normally justify their behavior by claiming that they are motivating others. ("If I wasn't after him all the time, nothing would get accomplished.") They often treat themselves as badly as they do other people. ("I can't believe I could have been so stupid.") This generates a level of chronic conflict, both internal and external, that becomes a principal source of stress.

Perfectionism is so common among recovering people that its antidotes have become AA slogans: "Live and Let Live" and "K.I.S.S." (Keep It Simple, Stupid).

Suggested exercises.

1. Sit down and write out a list of what you regard as your principal *weaknesses*—the areas where you are most disappointed in yourself.
2. Sit down and write a list of the principal weaknesses you have identified in the people around you—especially your loved ones and family members.
3. Go over the list with a counselor or sponsor. See if you can identify any attitudes that might create potential conflict

with others, or might lead you to be dissatisfied with yourself.

4. For each identified attitude, think of an *alternative* to your present perfectionism—another way of looking at the situation in a more positive light, which might reduce the chances for conflict. Discuss these with your counselor or sponsor.

Category B: Frustration Tolerance

Addicts are famous for impatience. They want it all *now,* no matter what the obstacles. If things don't improve according to their expectations, they often brood, worry, and get angry—which makes everything worse. Note that most of the slogans heard at Twelve Step meetings ("Easy Does It," "One Day at a Time") reflect the need for patience.

Suggested exercises:

1. Write out a list of what you expect from yourself and from other people over the next three to six months. The list should look like this:

I expect	By Date	Chance of Success
• To lose 20 pounds.	March 16	50%?
• To regain my driver's license	April 30	75%

2. When you're finished, go over your list with a counselor or sponsor. Evaluate your estimates for *realism:* Can you accomplish what you think you can in the time span you have allotted for yourself? What unforeseen circumstances might interfere with your goals?

3. Repeat steps one and two every three months. Ask yourself if you have set unreasonable goals for yourself in the past. How could you avoid repeating your mistake?

Category C: Obsessive Worry

It's normal to worry about problems, but if we're not careful, worry becomes a form of magical thinking. We convince ourselves that if we worry about something enough, it won't happen. But worrying itself has absolutely no effect on events, except to make us miserable, interfere with sleep and concentration, and distract us from taking actions that really will make a difference in our lives. The obsessive person must learn that certain events are out of our control, and that this is all right. The relevant AA slogan is "Let Go and Let God."

Suggested exercises:

1. Take two pieces of paper. On one, make a list of all the things in your life over which you believe you have ultimate control. On the other, list those facets of life you feel you cannot control.
2. Share your list with a counselor or sponsor. Discuss whether or not your lists are realistic. Do you find yourself trying to control things you can't reasonably expect to control? How do you put yourself in that position?
3. Now, make a list of specific problems you are afraid might happen in the next three months. Go over this list with the sponsor or counselor. How realistic is your anxiety? Suppose your worst fears came to pass? What would be the best way to handle it?
4. Spend time working on Steps Two and Three of the Twelve Steps. Discuss these with other group members whenever you can.

Category D: Resentments

Resentment is a form of anger held over time and most often arising from a situation in which you felt victimized, taken advantage of, or prejudiced against. Addicts and alcoholics develop a number of resentments during the course of their addiction, partly because they find themselves in conflict with others and partly because they externalize the causes of their drinking or drug use onto those around them.

Resentments are a major source of stress in recovery. The Fourth through Ninth Steps deal in part with identifying and resolving various resentments.

Suggested exercises:

1. Make a list of situations where you feel you have been victimized or unfairly taken advantage of, or have suffered from prejudicial treatment.
2. Share this list with your sponsor or counselor. Discuss the relative legitimacy of your feelings.
3. Talk about resentments at Step Meetings having to do with the Fourth through the Ninth Steps. Ask others how they dealt with resentments. Did any of them use resentments as an excuse to relapse? What happened as a result? Did drinking or drug use lessen the resentment?
4. Ask your sponsor or counselor whether you're ready for a Fourth and Fifth Step. If they believe you are, do it with their assistance.

Category E: Mistrust

Alcoholics and addicts can be among the most mistrustful people on earth. Part of this is due to the deceit and manipulation they were forced to practice during their active addiction: you may assume that everyone else's motives were as selfish as your own. This residual cynicism can lead you to misinterpret the behavior of counselors and other people in the recovering community and isolate you from their support. That's unfortunate, because in the first months of recovery, an alcoholic alone is an alcoholic in distress. Relevant AA slogan: "Keep Coming Back."

Suggested exercises:

1. Make at least one new acquaintance at every AA or NA meeting you attend. Tell this person a little about yourself; give them a chance to share some of their story.
2. Discuss your experiences with your sponsor or counselor. Do you find yourself suspicious of people's motives? What are you afraid will happen if you trust them? What are reasonable expectations in terms of trusting another person? What would be an unreasonable degree of trust?

Exercise Two: Practicing Stress Control with Brain Television

Here are some practical exercises for using visualization to alter your perspective on events and to help lessen the stress you experience.

The History of Embarrassment

Turn on your brain TV. Get a picture of the controls: the volume on the left, so you can adjust the intensity and the sound. The dial for switching channels is on the right.

Let a picture appear on the screen: it's *This Is Your Life* again, an episode called "Embarrassment." See the title flash across the screen. Oh, yeah, this is the episode where you relive some real embarrassing moments. Don't worry; it's going to turn out well.

Pick an embarrassing moment from the last couple of years. Got one? You don't? Who are you kidding?

Take your time. See yourself in the situation that made you feel embarrassed. Now, let yourself experience the embarrassment. The feeling in your stomach, if there was any. The feeling in your chest. The feeling in your face. You don't have to get into it too far, or force anything. Just enough to get in touch with the way it felt to be embarrassed.

Okay, reach down to the volume knob with your left hand. Now turn the knob slowly to the right, which will make it more intense. The feeling of embarrassment should be growing a little more acute. Now stop and reverse the knob. Turn it to the left, and let it become less intense. Keep on turning the knob until you feel no embarrassment at all.

Now, let the screen fade to gray. Then let another scene come into focus. It's the time previous to the one in the last episode when you felt some of the same feelings. When you felt embarrassed. Take your time.

Got it? Now, do the same thing with the volume control: first making it a little more intense, then reducing it until it's completely gone. The feeling has once again disappeared.

Let the screen fade to gray. Then bring it back into focus, this time on an episode from your childhood, when you felt embarrassed.

Repeat the procedure. Use the volume knob to reduce the intensity, then let the screen fade to gray. Bring up another image, from an earlier time in your life. Lower the intensity. Let the screen fade. Keep doing it until you're at a point where you don't think you can go further back. Until you're at the earliest point in your life where you can recall the feeling you associate with embarrassment.

Now do the same thing with that experience. Reduce it in intensity until the feeling is gone.

When it's gone, turn off the TV and let your eyes open as soon as you're ready.

You just learned to reduce stress. Embarrassment is an easy form of stress to identify, because everyone experiences it and people usually don't feel that that's unnatural. You can use the same technique with anger, anxiety, and nervous tension. Just identify the feeling, trace it back to a particular experience (you needn't go all the way back, just far enough to ground the feeling in your experience), intensify and then reduce it.

When you get the technique down, you can use it on situations that just happened. When you start to feel the feelings or sensations that you associate with stress—irritability, anxiety, whatever—just take a moment to relax, turn on your brain television, picture the scene that's bothering you, and use your volume control to turn it down.

Half-Empty/Half-Full

This is a variation on the old adage that you can look at a glass as half-empty or half-full. Suppose you went through a painful divorce a couple of years ago, and haven't found the nerve to start dating again. At first, it was because of lingering ties to the old relationship, but now you're afraid that you've forgotten how to have a sexual relationship with someone. The problem: *uncertainty.* You've got two ways to look at it:

Half-Empty: you worry about how you look to the other person—whether or not he or she likes you, is attracted to you, respects you.

Half-Full: you think about all the interesting new people you get to meet—one might even turn out to be fascinating enough to fall in love with.

1. Make a list of problems you're worried about.
2. Divide another sheet of paper into two columns, one entitled "Half-Empty," the other "Half-Full."
3. Under "Half-Empty," enter what you're afraid of, in regard to each problem.
4. Under "Half-Full," enter something about the same situation that represents an opportunity for you.
5. Do this for all your problems. Memorize the half-full list.
6. When you find yourself thinking of a problem in terms of a

"half-empty," remind yourself about the "half-full" opportunity.

Brain TV to the Rescue

This is an exercise in acting-as-if, or *modeling*. In other words, if there's a problem you think you can't handle, then think of someone you know who can, and borrow that personality for a little while.

Turn on your brain TV. Put a picture on the screen of something you're afraid of. Asking for a raise, for example; most people have trouble with that.

Picture yourself doing it. Pretty pathetic, huh? Almost like you think your boss is right to turn you down.

Okay, now picture someone you know who's a lot more assertive than you are. Picture this person going through the same process. They're good at it, aren't they?

Now put the two pictures on the screen at the same time. It isn't hard; it's like those divided images in the Olympics, which they use so you can simultaneously watch volleyball and rhythmic gymnastics. You, however, don't have to follow both at the same time. Look at one, then the other. Compare the two. Start to merge them together, with your image beginning to take on some of the assertive traits of the more assertive person. Experiment a little. Put his or her voice in your mouth. Adopt some of his or her body posture and presentation. Steal some of the arguments that you think are impressive. As your image becomes stronger, let it grow to fill the whole screen, as the image of your model shrinks, fades off into a lower corner, then disappears completely.

Now it's just you again. Replay the whole scene from the beginning, starting with you going into the boss's office and asking for a raise, using your new, improved personality. Any better? If you want, start the process again, using a different model. Maybe someone assertive from TV or the movies.

You can use this exercise for almost any anxiety-provoking situation. It's called *modeling*. You're simply taking on some traits that you need to accomplish a specific task.

THE SIXTH TRAP: COMPLACENCY

"That (drugs) is all behind me now. I don't want to dwell on the past."

—Professional athlete, three weeks sober

From a strictly medical perspective, alcoholism and drug dependency are remarkably simple to arrest. First, you abandon alcohol and drugs long enough to undergo withdrawal and restore yourself to something resembling normal function. From that point on, it's largely a matter of not going backward. That's a lot less complicated than what the diabetic or heart patient faces. Its very simplicity gives you a better chance of survival.

But there's a drawback to having a disease that can be arrested but not cured: while it's under control, it's all too easy to forget what life was like when it wasn't. You can lose sight of the fact that you still have the disease.

This is bad, because then you'll stop treating it. The minute you do, the possibility of relapse immediately increases. This is why complacency is as much the enemy of recovery as stress. And it's why clinicians worry as much about an alcoholic who experiences too *few* difficulties as they do about one who experiences too many.

Medicine operates on a practical equation: *more symptoms = more treatment*. Conversely, a decrease in symptoms means a reduction in treatment. That's why your physician or psychiatrist admits you to the hospital when you're at your sickest and discharges you as soon as you're better. Makes perfect sense, doesn't it? Except that there is a third line in the equation, often unspoken: *no symptoms = no treatment.*

Suppose you went to your doctor and asked him for help with an illness that had been in remission for the past three years. He'd look at you suspiciously. His whole frame of reference is to identify and treat symptoms. In their absence, he really wouldn't know what to do with you. He'd simply advise you to return if the condition worsens.

But what if the treatment is keeping the symptoms at bay? Then your role as the patient becomes more important than the doctor's. You must continue to administer the treatment regimen—even something as simple as attending Twelve Step meetings—as long as you live. There are no holidays.

If you allow yourself to become complacent, you'll probably forget that.

ATTITUDE CHECK #6: COMPLACENCY

To meaure your tendency toward complacency, answer yes or no to the following statements.

1. I think I have really learned my lesson, and I can't imagine any situation in which I would drink or use drugs.
2. I believe that everyone has to recover in his own way, and what works for one person isn't necessarily good for another.
3. Relapse is the least of my worries right now.
4. I believe that there are other things in life besides staying sober, and they're important, too.
5. I feel I have a good handle on my own récovery.
6. I don't think I'll ever drink or use drugs again.
7. Counselors and sponsors are often unreasonable in their demands.

8. I think if you're secure within yourself you can handle almost anything.
9. Once I make up my mind, I never change it.
10. I feel I have my sobriety well in hand and it's time for me to move on to other issues and problems.
11. I no longer worry about relapse.
12. I don't want to become a fanatic about recovery.

Look at the box below for an interpretation of the results.

If you answered "yes" to three or less of the questions your chance of relapse is low. If you answered "yes" to between four and six of the questions, your chance of relapse is moderate and you should continue to learn and be aware of the pitfalls of recovery. If you answered "yes" to between seven and nine of the questions you are at high risk for relapse and should pay particular attention to this trap. If you answered "yes" to ten or more of the questions you are in a relapse "red zone" and need to seek and follow good advice immediately.

HOW MUCH IS ENOUGH?

The internal dialogue that paves the way for complacency actually appears early in recovery. As you begin to feel better, you wonder if the hard part isn't already over. Why not cut back on the time and attention you devote to staying sober? *After all, you tell yourself, I'm on the right track. Doing well. Isn't it reasonable that I should turn some of my energy elsewhere?*

The crisis that drove you into treatment is past. The pain of withdrawal is only a memory. Your cravings, once so persistent, have begun to wax and wane. You understood that you had to work hard to get sober. But what about when things come easily?

In fact, it occurs to you that the only reason you're sticking with the program is because somebody has told you that if you don't, you'll fail.

But of course, *you* don't know that. And things are different now. In the early days of sobriety, you were weak; you needed all the help you could get. Now you're strong. Strong enough, perhaps, to cut back on those meetings. Strong enough to test yourself against temptation. It's not as though you plan to drink again. You don't even want a drink. All you want is to live your life in a more reasonable fashion.

Seductive, isn't it? You don't even have to make a conscious decision to return to alcohol or drugs. You just stop doing the things that stand between you and your addiction. Sooner or later, life sends along a problem you can't handle, and off you go again.

Sometimes this is done under the banner of reasonableness. Admittedly, total abstinence may seem like an unreasonable demand to the newly recovering. After all, these substances have been the central focus of life for months, years, perhaps decades. Just the change in lifestyle required by sobriety is monumental.

So in that respect, the addict is right. At its core, recovery demands an act of faith and persistence that cannot be compared to anything else in daily life. If somewhere along the line you forget this, relapse is sure to follow.

HOW THE TRAP CLOSES

Let's look at the reasoning process that leads into this trap.

The underlying assumption: That superficial success negates the
    need for further effort.

Resulting behavior: You begin to drop various recovery-related
    activities, such as attending meetings or talking with a
    sponsor.

The second decision: Since reducing your program didn't automatically result in relapse, you interpret this as proof that you were right.

Resulting behavior: You begin to look for other ways to reduce the time and effort you devote to staying sober.

The third decision: Having grown more confident, you abandon the majority of your recovery-oriented activities.

Resulting behavior: You are now doing very little (if anything) to protect yourself against relapse.

The fourth decision: Because other people (family members, counselors, AA friends, et cetera) question your decisions, you decide to avoid them or to make this a forbidden topic of discussion. ("It's really none of your business— I'm fine.")

Resulting behavior: You further lower your awareness of the disease and the possibility of relapse.

The fifth decision: You decide to take on additional problems or responsibilities, based on your view of yourself as being "well."

Resulting behavior: The number of problems in your life begins to increase.

The sixth decision: You question the need to avoid alcohol and drugs *entirely.*

Resulting behavior: You reintroduce them into your life— whether gradually, as an experiment, or all at once, due to some external crisis. Relapse has occurred.

RED FLAGS

Watch out for these phrases if they begin to show up in your thinking or conversation:

1. "I can't understand what these people expect of me. I have a life of my own to live."
2. "It isn't fair to ask me to spend the rest of my days under the gun. Watched, monitored. You're treating me like a child."
3. "It's your constant nagging that makes me want to go out and get high."
4. "I'm doing fine on my own. If I was in some kind of trouble, then I could understand the concern."
5. "I've got nothing against AA, but the fact is I'm doing very well, especially under the circumstances. There comes a time when you have to stand on your own two feet. Besides, talking about drinking makes me want to drink."
6. "I've got problems, sure, but they've got nothing to do with alcohol or drugs. And they need my attention."
7. "Drinking is the least of my worries right now."

RELAPSE IN ACTION

Dan Perry and the Drunk-Driving Arrest

In the following case, note how an alcoholic takes apart his recovery program "brick by brick," simply because he thinks he no longer needs it.

It was after the third DWI ("driving while intoxicated" arrest) that Dan Perry began to suspect that something might be wrong with his drinking. He resolved that this kind of thing would not happen again.

So for Dan, the fourth DWI had the quality of a religious experience. He had no recollection whatsoever of the circumstances in which he was arrested. Second, he was forced to spend

30 days in an alcoholism program. Third, he spent 30 additional days in jail.

Somewhere during this span, Dan made up his mind to quit drinking. To his surprise, Dan found he liked AA, and found sobriety easy. The rest of his life was going better than expected: his lawyer had worked out a deal where if Dan remained under supervision for a year, he could get his record wiped clean.

Dan was pretty much pleased with the way things were going—except his AA sponsor was on him about his Fourth Step.

Dan's sponsor felt that Dan wasn't taking it seriously enough. They argued about it much of the time. "Look," Dan argued, "what are you making such a big deal for? I haven't had a drink in months. I'm going to meetings. I see people at these meetings who have been sober a lot longer than me, who aren't doing half as well. So why are you on my case?"

Dan went on as before. He dropped his original sponsor and found a new one who wasn't as demanding.

A few months later, Dan got an opportunity to pick up a few extra shifts at his job, which would allow him to pay off some of his debts. He jumped at the chance. Of course, it also limited his AA involvement to one or two meetings every week.

"It's only for a short period," Dan explained to his friends. "Six or seven weeks at the most. I'm sick of these creditors hassling me on the phone. I just want to get out from under this debt."

But even his new sponsor thought fewer meetings was a bad idea. "You're not even a year sober, Dan. You could get depressed again, and find yourself wanting to drink. Why don't we do a Fifth Step? You've got some sobriety under your belt. Things are going well at work and with your financial problems. Sounds like a perfect opportunity."

Dan begged off. After that, he and his sponsor lost touch. It wasn't that Dan set out deliberately to avoid him. It was simply that his other responsibilities took up a lot of his time, and he usually arrived home too late in the evening to return phone calls.

Besides, there were other things to worry about. Like his probation program, with its twice-weekly monitoring schedule. It was inconvenient, and did nothing whatsoever to help Dan's self-esteem.

Dan expressed these sentiments to his probation officer. It led to their first big argument.

"Your attendance at Aftercare is lousy, Dan," the P.O. said. "I can't imagine how you manage to stay sober. I'm going to have to tell the judge you're not following his instructions."

Dan was furious. "That's a lie! It's like nothing is ever good enough for you people!"

"That's not the point."

"It *is* the point! I'm off alcohol, and you're hassling me as if I was still drinking! This is harassment!" He stood up. "I don't think we have anything more to talk about. Tell the judge whatever you like. My lawyer will appeal it. There are other judges, you know, and other probation officers. I have rights."

True to his word, Dan instructed his attorney to appeal. Based on Dan's record to date and the testimony of a psychiatrist whose help Dan had enlisted, the probation was revoked. Dan was a free man.

A week later, he received a letter from the Internal Revenue Service, telling him he owed $6,000 in back taxes. If he didn't pay, he faced criminal charges.

That night, he woke from a sound sleep with a titanic craving for a drink. He couldn't remember feeling anything to compare with it. He reached for the phone to call his sponsor, then stopped as he put the receiver to his ear.

God, I can't call him, after all the things I've said, Dan thought. He couldn't call the treatment center, either. *They'd just want to stick me in the hospital, and I can't afford it.*

I can handle this, he told himself, even as the sweat poured off his forehead and the image of a cool bottle of vodka hung on the edge of his thoughts. *I have to handle this.*

After a moment he felt better. Discovering he was out of cigarettes, he threw on some clothes and drove down toward the center of town, looking for something open at one o'clock in the morning. The only thing he saw was a bar.

He felt the ribbon of tension in his spine. His heart beat loud and fast.

Well, I guess they probably sell smokes . . . I'll just run in and run out.

Three weeks later, Dan quit drinking once again. This time in jail. With drunk-driving arrest number five.

CO-DEPENDENT ROLE IN THIS TRAP

Oddly, friends and family members often fall prey to the same sense of complacency as the addict. They too are lulled into a false feeling of security by superficial success. Even if it contradicts their own past experience.

Dan's wife, Adrienne, is a good example. When Dan first began missing his treatment sessions, the counselor called to seek her support.

"I don't know why you're calling me," Adrienne told her. "There's nothing I can do about it. He's promised to stay sober. I have to believe him."

"Hasn't he gone back on that promise before?" the counselor asked.

"Lots of times," she responded. "But I have to believe that this time things will be different. I don't have any choice."

In reality, Adrienne was exercising her power of choice at

that very moment. She chose to pretend that Dan was all right and that his word alone was reliable assurance of sobriety—even though she knew this to be untrue. If asked, she might characterize this as "loyalty" to her husband. But it's really a form of denial. When you're afraid of what might lie beneath the surface, you can always refuse to look.

HOW TO AVOID THIS TRAP

This is one of the most difficult traps to avoid, because we normally associate relapse with problems, and this trap hinges on their *absence*. So we'll begin with two simple exercises to get in touch with the possibility of failure.

Exercise One: A Trip Through Our Personal History

Our brains are good at "forgetting" painful experiences. If they weren't, women would probably never have more than one child. But sometimes we forget too much. There are certain experiences we'd do better to remember.

Turn on your brain TV. Remember you have a control knob on the left that allows you to adjust the volume and the screen brightness. On the right you have a channel changer. If at any point you're uncomfortable with what you see on the screen, just change the channel.

Now, picture yourself on the screen, the way you looked on the day you stopped drinking or using drugs. Got the picture? Note the clothes you were wearing, the way your hair looked, the furniture in the room. Where were you? In a treatment program? At a clinic? In the hospital? At an AA meeting? At home, suffering by yourself?

Replay as much of that day as you can. What happened, who you talked with, what they said. The furnishings in the room, things like that. Flesh out your memory of that particular day. Watch yourself on the screen.

Now, pretend you're an interviewer (perhaps your favorite roving reporter). You've been dispatched to the scene to interview yourself the way you were on that particular day. Ask your past self the kind of questions you imagine a journalist might ask. *How do you feel? What motivates you to quit at this time? Do you think you'll succeed? What if you fail? Are you afraid of anything?* Listen to the answers.

Got it? Okay, now blank the screen. Replace it with a picture of a point in time, during your active addiction, when you were at your absolute lowest emotionally. If you have trouble locating it, look for a feeling of hopelessness and desperation. Picture where you were when you felt that way. What you were doing. Who was with you, if anyone. Again, flesh it out. If the feelings become too intense, just flip the channel.

Done? Now, interview yourself, just as you did earlier. Ask the image on the screen how it feels—listen to the answers. Do you feel sorry for your past self?

Got it? Blank the screen once again. This time, picture yourself looking the way you do right now.

When that's done, blank the screen once more. Divide the screen into three sections. In the section on the left, put the picture of you at the lowest point in your addiction. In the right-hand section, put an image of yourself on the day you gave up alcohol and drugs. And in the middle, put the image of yourself as you are now.

When you've done that, study the three images. Compare and contrast them. What are the differences between the way you look now and the way you looked then?

Turn off your brain television. Get a pen and paper and write down a brief summary of your experience. Note the differences between how you felt on the day you quit drinking and at your lowest and highest points. Isn't it interesting how things can change—for better or for worse?

Exercise Two: The Future Gone Wrong

Once again, turn on your brain TV. Picture the control knobs on the left and right. If you become nervous about what's on the screen, switch the channel. It will disappear instantly.

Imagine yourself waking up in the morning after a relapse. You're in bed. Look around you. Where are you? At home? In a hospital?

How do you feel? Do a little check of your various body systems: stomach, head, et cetera. Got any aches and pains?

Now, blank the screen. Replace the image of yourself in bed with a picture of yourself explaining your relapse to someone important to you. A spouse, a child, a parent, a boss, a close friend, a sponsor. Listen to the explanations you give. Do they sound like excuses? What is the expression on the face of the person you're talking with? Listen to what they say in response.

Repeat that scene with a different person. Is it any different?

When you're done, shut off your brain TV and write out a short summary of what happened.

Exercise Three: Renewing Your Self-Diagnosis

1. Take steps to "renew" your original self-diagnosis. Repeat periodically the brain TV exercise at the conclusion of the second trap. Share the results with your sponsor, counselor, or another knowledgeable person. Are you aware of symptoms you may have experienced but didn't include in your original self-diagnosis?

2. Commit yourself to a certain level of recovery-oriented activity, *whether or not you think you need it.*

When you went through treatment, you probably made commitments to attend a certain number of meetings and to do a certain number of activities specifically to avoid relapse. Sit down and take an inventory: How well have you kept these commitments?

Have you fallen prey to the "New Year's Resolution" syndrome? Are you doing the things you said you needed to? Or have you let most of your program drop, so that the only thing standing between you and relapse is your own willpower?

Discuss this inventory with your counselor or another knowledgeable person. Actively seek their feedback.

(Hint: you won't want to do this. You'll want to correct the problem on your own. Don't; get outside advice. Trust us.)

SIX THINGS TO HELP YOU REMEMBER YOUR DISEASE

1. Make a point of volunteering to speak at an AA, NA, or CA Step meeting.
2. If you're shy about speaking to the group, then share your story one on one.
3. Find a newcomer and make a point of sharing your experience of addiction. After all, the best way to learn is to teach.
4. Volunteer for a "job" within the fellowship: secretary of a meeting, program chairman, et cetera.
5. Spend time around AA clubs or, if possible, volunteer at a detox unit.
6. Keep a journal of your recovery. Each day, write down something you did to help yourself stay sober.

LIVING WITH A CHRONIC DISEASE

Addictive disease, by its very nature, imposes certain limits on its victims. Because it's *chronic,* you must continue to treat it even after the obvious signs disappear. Because it's *primary,* you must learn to identify its symptoms independent of the circumstances that surround them. Because it's *progressive,* you can't ignore it; the longer you do, the more you'll suffer. And because it's potentially *fatal,* your life is at stake.

But alcoholism isn't the only illness in this category. A number of medical conditions operate in similar fashion; cancer, heart disease, and diabetes are just a few of the better known examples.

Many psychiatric disorders—schizophrenia and some forms of depression and anxiety, for example—are also chronic by nature.

Imagine then what life is like when you are forced to treat not only addiction but also a chronic medical or psychiatric disorder. Complicates things, doesn't it? That's the essence of the seventh and eighth traps.

And of course, even in the absence of other illnesses, your poor battered brain must recover from previous damage done by alcohol and drugs. Suppose sobriety finds you struggling with an unforeseen yet persistent problem like insomnia, migraine headaches, sexual dysfunction? Still another complication that, unaddressed, could contribute to relapse. That's the focus of the ninth trap.

Read on.

THE SEVENTH TRAP:
MEDICAL PROBLEMS DURING RECOVERY

"I resented the fact that I had finally given up alcohol and drugs, and here was some moron with a medical degree telling me I might die anyway. I was surprised to find I wanted to live."

—Recovering alcoholic
being treated for cancer

"Chronic pain is like a lousy marriage. It looks ugly in the morning, spoiling your breakfast. It interrupts you at work. It meets you at the door when you get home. It nags you about all the things you were supposed to do and forgot. It's the last thing you see when you go to bed, and it wakes you up in the middle of the night just to let you know it's still there."

—Chronic pain patient, age 33

One of the most unfair things about alcoholism and drug dependence—and these are inherently unfair conditions to begin with—is that you may also suffer from other diseases at the same time.

Many alcoholics and addicts have heart conditions, diabetes, emphysema, cancer, orthopedic problems, arthritis, brain tumors. In some instances, alcoholism played a role in bringing about these disorders. In others, it's largely coincidental.

Thus a common scenario for relapse involves an addict faced with the prospect of treating more than one chronic disease. Sometimes relapse occurs because the addict doesn't recognize the existence of the second disorder, or, for one reason or another, fails to treat it. Sometimes, it's due to the fact that medical science has yet to develop a good treatment for a particular illness. And not infrequently, it's because the treatment for one problem provokes relapse in another.

No matter what the situation, the alcoholic or addict with medical problems is unusually vulnerable. It requires considerable thought and planning to avoid relapse.

ATTITUDE CHECK #7: COEXISTING MEDICAL PROBLEMS

To find out if your attitudes make you unusually vulnerable to relapse due to coexisting medical problems, answer yes or no to the following statements.

For those who already have chronic medical problems:

1. I am concerned that my other medical problems might interfere with my ability to stay off alcohol or drugs.
2. One of my reasons for drinking or drug use was physical discomfort associated with medical problems.
3. I suffer from chronic pain.
4. I feel that if people understood how bad I felt sometimes, they would know why I used drugs (alcohol).

5. I feel that my doctors underestimate the discomfort I experience.

For those not currently being treated for a chronic medical problem:

1. I have a low tolerance for physical discomfort.
2. I have great difficulty accepting any limitations on my
   activities.
3. I usually put off going to the doctor until I absolutely have
   to.
4. I am very frightened by the idea that I might become
   seriously ill.
5. I think if I ever got cancer or some other serious illness, I
   might just kill myself.

Look at the box below for an interpretation of the results.

> If you answered "yes" to one of the questions your
> chance of relapse is low. If you answered "yes" to
> two of the questions your chance of relapse is
> moderate and you should continue to learn, and
> be aware of, the pitfalls of recovery. If you an-
> swered "yes" to 3 of the questions you are at high
> risk for relapse and should pay particular attention
> to this trap. If you answered "yes" to four or more
> of the questions you are in a relapse "red zone"
> and need to seek and follow good advice imme-
> diately.

HOW THE TRAP CLOSES

This particular trap depends on your willingness to make several
key assumptions.

First, that certain symptoms brought about or related to

medical problems—principally pain, anxiety, or discomfort—can be effectively, if temporarily, treated with alcohol or drugs.

Second, that this is true even for people with a history of addictive disease.

Third—and this is crucial—that whatever pain you experience comes from your medical condition and not from drug withdrawal.

Fourth, that medical problems can be so painful that a return to alcoholism or drug addiction is therefore justifiable.

Once the assumptions have been made, the trap closes in the following fashion:

The first decision: That your medical problem cannot be treated effectively.

Resulting behavior: Discouragement with treatment.

The second decision: Decides to turn away from search for new or alternate treatments.

Resulting behavior: Sense of hopelessness about eventual relief.

The third decision: Focused on somatic symptoms and discomfort, you look only for temporary relief.

Resulting behavior: Craving increases for addictive drug.

The fourth decision: You decide that discomfort is unendurable and worth any effort to relieve, no matter what the cost.

Resulting behavior: Reintroduces addictive drug; relapse.

What the doctor sees: escalating complaints about pain or discomfort because a medical disorder is not responding fast enough to treatments to suit the patient. You find yourself concentrating on these symptoms to the exclusion of recovery-related activities. It isn't long before you lose sight of your addictive history and reintroduce the drug. One pathway: you begin with a milder substitute (often cross-addictive) but then find a reason to return to your drug of choice or something of equal potency.

Emotionally, this pattern is marked by extreme self-absorption. Feelings of anger, resentment, and self-pity predominate, and are coupled with a profound worry about the outcome. You may find yourself questioning your values and the meaning of your life. You might *somaticize* your anxiety into new symptoms that you interpret as a sign the illness is growing worse, which you use to justify more medication, or even a return to alcohol and other drugs.

RED FLAGS

If you're under treatment for a medical problem and find the following sentiments dominating your thoughts, watch out.

1. "There's no way I can tolerate this."
2. "You can't understand what it's like to live with this."
3. "What's the point of being clean if I feel like this?"
4. "What am I supposed to do? They've tried everything, and none of it works."
5. "How do you expect me to go to work or to function or to live a normal life without something for this problem?"
6. "They can't even guarantee I'm going to live. What's the point of staying sober?"
7. "If I can just get through this one night . . . just this one occasion . . . I can stop tomorrow."

RELAPSE IN ACTION

Medical problems come in more than one form. Accordingly, we offer two examples.

The First Pattern: Refusing to treat your medical problems

Some people are as stubborn about treating medical disorders as they are about getting help for alcoholism.

The Story of Angus P.

Angus's diabetes presented no problem in terms of medical management. But the doctors left one factor out of the equation: Angus. He simply refused to follow recommendations when it came to diabetes.

The struggle began in the alcoholism ward of the local hospital. Angus adamantly refused to eat the food prepared by the hospital kitchen. The doctor reiterated the importance of adhering to the diet.

"Thank you, Doctor, but you can skip the lecture," said Angus. "I've already had it a million times. I've been diabetic for ten years, and eating whatever I please for the majority of that time, along with drinking a bottle of vodka every day. And as far as I can tell, I'm none the worse for wear. So if you don't mind, I'll trust my own experience rather than your advice."

So the chief of the hospital decided to meet with Angus the next morning after breakfast.

"I cannot understand you," the chief said, trying to look as authoritative as possible. "You've been diabetic for ten years. Why do you persist in acting as though you don't have that disease?"

"I know I have diabetes," Angus replied. "I'm not stupid. I've been through the courses, read all the books. I probably know as much about it as you do. I simply disagree with the treatment. If there were going to be a lot of damage done to my body by diabetes, it would have already occurred. Yet my own physician admits I'm in remarkable shape. So why should I give up food at the same time as I give up something else I enjoy—alcohol?"

The chief knew he was licked. "So what are your plans for the future?"

"Simple. I give up drinking, and take Antabuse. If I want ice cream, I will have ice cream."

Angus was discharged from the hospital a week later.

Three months afterward, he was readmitted to the hospital for detoxification. He met again with the hospital chief, who had assumed control of his case.

"I hope you're not going to say you told me so," Angus groaned.

"Of course not. I told you so."

"I suppose I deserve it. I just wasn't expecting what happened to me. I couldn't seem to keep my emotions in control. You have to understand, I have spent most of my life being in control. Never losing my temper, always measuring my responses. And all of a sudden, I was flying off the handle, throwing tantrums over nothing. And the depressions . . . I've never experienced anything like them. I thought I was beginning to go crazy. About a week ago, I started drinking. And I went on a binge, for the first time in my life."

"I think maybe you underestimated the impact your drinking was having on your diabetes," the chief said. "The alcohol probably kept you from realizing how much your blood sugar was fluctuating. You weren't prepared for the change once the alcohol was removed."

The Second Pattern: Treatment for one illness interferes with treatment of another.

Sometimes good medical care for one disease is bad medical care for a second disease.

The Story of Gwen N.

Gwen, a chronic back patient, developed a dependency on narcotics and muscle relaxants over the course of approximately three years of medical treatment. Gwen knew she was using more than the recommended dosages of painkillers and sedatives, but she felt her continual discomfort justified it, in addition to her "low tolerance for pain." Besides, her physicians never indicated a concern about her drug use, outside of a few mild admonishments to "cut back" a little.

So Gwen was completely surprised when her orthopedist called her into the office to discuss her use of medications. A week later, at his insistence, Gwen entered a detoxification program at the local hospital. To her surprise, she found she liked her two specialists who took over her case. The biofeedback exercises were relaxing—kind of like nap time in kindergarten—and the psychiatrist was easy to talk to, not at all condescending or aloof. She had a lot of problems with giving up the drugs, however. She couldn't sleep, had frequent back spasms, and a near-continual headache. Nevertheless, she was very glad she'd allowed herself to be talked into hospitalization. She knew there was no way she would have been able to tolerate this experience at home.

After two weeks, she was discharged to outpatient follow-up. She was to receive physical therapy three times weekly for three months, and visit her psychiatrist every Thursday morning. She was still quite anxious about what would happen to her now that she was off narcotics, but she was willing to give it a try.

And indeed, Gwen did better than expected. For a period of perhaps seven months, she kept up her regimen of physical and psychological therapy. There were continued problems, especially in the area of headache and lower-back pain, but relatively few crises. Gwen felt that, at long last, the end of the tunnel was in sight.

Then one night Gwen went to bed. In the middle of the night, she woke up from a sound sleep and realized she needed to go to the bathroom.

She was surprised to find she couldn't get out of bed.

She tried to sit up, and couldn't. She tried to roll over to slide out of bed onto her knees, and couldn't. She tried to reach up and turn on a light, and couldn't. Any move at all seemed to produce excruciating pain.

Gwen was in big trouble.

Gradually, with supreme effort, Gwen managed to roll out of bed onto her hands and knees. Several times, she screamed out loud with the pain. She began to crawl, a few inches at a time, toward the bathroom. It was twenty feet from where she began. She reached it in forty minutes.

Gwen was alert enough to turn on the hot water in the bathtub, and with a horrible effort managed to roll into the tub. The heat loosened her muscles enough to allow her to stand. She called the ambulance and waited for them to take her to the hospital. She stood for half an hour in the middle of the living room. She was afraid that if she sat she would be unable to stand again.

When she got to the emergency room, she dutifully told the doctor about her history of drug dependency. He seemed preoccupied.

GWEN: I have to be careful about medications. I shouldn't have any narcotics and I should probably not have Valium or any of that type muscle relaxant.

DOCTOR: Well, I think we'd better do whatever is necessary to relieve this spasm. We'll worry about the rest of it later.

So the doctor went ahead and gave Gwen a large dose of various narcotics and muscle relaxants. The spasm abated, and Gwen was resting peacefully the following day. She was discharged with a large prescription of Valium and Codeine.

After a month, she tried to stop taking them. She couldn't.

HOW TO AVOID THIS TRAP

Because this pattern is so closely related to certain underlying assumptions, let's begin by taking a look at one of them: the belief that reliance on drugs is an effective way—in fact, the *only* effective way—to deal with chronic pain.

THE MYTH OF ESCAPE
_____ FROM CHRONIC PAIN _____

People use painkillers and muscle relaxants for one reason: they lessen physical discomfort. But that simple equation disappears in the face of addictive disease. Once you become an addict, the same medications that once worked so effectively—and still work for your neighbors—become part of the problem rather than part of the solution.

Think of pain as the body's warning system. When nature wants us to stay away from something, she makes it painful. The pain network is vast and far-reaching, and includes not only the nerves that *produce* painful impulses, but also mechanisms designed to *suppress* pain once its usefulness is past.

For decades, scientists have known that the body has its own natural painkilling substances. There were always a number of clues. For instance, the effectiveness of a technique such as acupuncture, where needles inserted into various sites produce temporary relief. Obviously, the needles themselves hold no magic. Somehow, they must stimulate the body to produce something that suppresses pain—a natural narcotic of some type.

Or take victims of the most severe type of chronic pain—people so afflicted that they live in a state of constant anguish the rest of us can only see in nightmares. When certain areas of their brains are electrically stimulated, the pain vanishes, only to return when the stimulation ceases. Clearly, stimulation must cause the brain to produce a painkiller strong enough to eliminate even the most severe discomfort. Somehow, in these individuals, the brain has "forgotten" how to produce this substance on its own.

Evidence like this strongly suggests the presence of a "natural narcotic." The opiates—drugs like codeine, morphine, and heroin—must tap into this natural painkilling system, activating the release of chemicals that suppress pain. And in fact, that's exactly what happens.

Now let's switch for a minute to the subject of *chronic* pain, the kind that lingers long after the injury that brought it about has faded. Our key painkilling medicines—such as the narcotics—are designed to deal with *acute* pain, related to a specific condition and a known cause. Chronic pain, by comparison, is often of unknown origin. You feel pain, but your doctor isn't sure why. And the longer this situation continues, the more frustrating it is for all concerned.

"It still hurts," you insist, while the doctor shakes his head. "It must be some kind of nerve problem," he tells you. "I can't find anything on the X rays, the scans, that would cause it. . . ."

That's chronic pain: the bane of physical medicine, the most likely to require long-term treatment with narcotics or muscle relaxants, and the most apt to lead to addiction. Naturally, because drugs seem so effective in providing relief, the pain patient becomes convinced they are an absolute necessity. But then something happens. Addictive disease changes the rules.

When scientists first discovered the body's natural painkillers (called endorphins), they hoped to use their new knowledge to develop safe, nonaddictive drugs. We could remove some of the painkilling substances from our bodies and store them for use when we suffered an injury.

Unfortunately, subjects given their own endorphin substances developed tolerance and dependence just as they did when given morphine or heroin. The key variable wasn't whether the drug was "natural" or manufactured, but instead whether or not it came from *outside* us.

No one knows why this is true. Apparently, the body's regulating mechanisms don't always understand how to handle narcotics. Sometimes, its reaction to foreign painkillers is simply to shut down its own painkilling mechanisms. That produces a deficit in natural painkillers which can only be repaired by increasing the dose of the drug. In other words, you're left with a greater deficit than before you took the medication. Which means you'll have to increase your ration of morphine or heroin or whatever just to get the same effect. It also means the body will call out for additional medication should you for any reason interrupt the supply.

How does the body call for a painkiller? With pain, of course. And as your own natural mechanisms begin once again to produce painkillers, the pain diminishes. We call that a withdrawal syndrome. And the condition which produces it is known as drug addiction.

Withdrawal is the wild card in pain management. When you're dependent on a drug to the point where falling blood levels bring on withdrawal symptoms, then you're no longer taking the drug for whatever illness originally caused your pain. You're taking it to relieve withdrawal. Ironically, withdrawal symptoms include the same ones that normally mark an acute flare-up of your illness. And if there is any legitimate pain going on at that moment, withdrawal will augment and sustain it, making it more difficult to endure.

When this happens, the addict is faced with a dilemma. It *feels* as though his medical problems have worsened. He has always operated on the assumption that pain is the enemy and medication his principal ally. And yet, there's growing evidence that pain may no longer be the major problem at all—drug dependence has replaced it.

But the only way to know for sure is to do the one thing the addict is most afraid of: go off the medication completely. And that will bring about a period of somewhat increased pain, followed by a post-acute period of waxing and waning pain—neither of which the addict wants to face. It's easier to put the whole thing off, to keep taking the medications, to continue to resist any suggestion that drugs could be a problem. That's why most addicted medical patients seek help only at the insistence of their doctors, when drug use has escalated to a point where the doctor is frightened they'll overdose. And it's why continuing medical problems are a major cause of relapse in some patients.

Do narcotics and muscle relaxants provide escape from pain for someone who has become addicted? Only if the pain is largely withdrawal-related. Even then, the relief is temporary, and when the pain returns, it may be worse than before.

CO-DEPENDENT ROLE IN THIS TRAP

Our impulse is to offer help and solace to people who are sick, and no one is better at this than the co-dependent. A natural caretaker, the co-dependent finds it extremely difficult to deal with addiction when the alcoholic or addict is also experiencing some type of medical problem. More than once, our efforts to detoxify a severely addicted chronic-pain patient have been met with angry resistance on the part of a spouse. In one case, a woman sought our help because her husband had taken so many narcotics and benzodiazepine tranquilizers that he was unable to walk and simply collapsed unconscious on the living room floor. When we began detoxification, however, he quite naturally began to complain of various aches and pains. His orthopedist reassured him that this was normal and quite harmless, but his wife came storming into our office to complain that we were "taking him down too fast." Even slowing down the timetable for withdrawal failed to pacify her; she insisted we were not sufficiently concerned with her husband's anguish. Finally, she picked him up in the middle of the night and took him home from the hospital. The next day, she called to inform us that she was seeking other guidance and was going to try regulating his consumption of medicines herself. Later, we heard from his original orthopedist that he had died of an overdose a few months after our last contact.

SOME SUGGESTIONS FOR DEALING WITH MEDICAL PROBLEMS IN RECOVERY

1. Pick Your Physician. This is probably the most important. You can't assume that physicians who haven't had specific training in addictions—no matter how skilled they might otherwise be—understand the dangers inherent in dealing with addictive disease.

We used to tell our patients to take only certain medications that we thought would not "wake up" the craving for alcohol and drugs. But we realized later that it is extremely difficult to be treated for any major medical procedure without receiving these substances.

We had occasion to take a friend of ours to the hospital, a recovering alcoholic with twenty-five years' sobriety in AA. He was going in for routine back surgery. The admitting nurse took his history and then, not ten minutes after we arrived, while we were sitting there chatting amiably, brought him a cup with a pill in it.

"Take this," she said, smiling.

"What is it?" he asked.

"Xanax. It's a muscle relaxant."

"You know I don't take tranquilizers? That I'm a recovering alcoholic? Haven't touched a drop in twenty-five years."

"Well, this is a muscle relaxant. The doctor ordered it."

"I'd rather not. I'm not tense."

"You have to take it, sir. The doctor ordered it."

"But I don't take pills unless they're absolutely necessary."

"This is absolutely necessary. You have to take it."

"Well, all right, then. If you're sure."

Now as far as we know, there is no reason a patient who is sitting calmly in his room thinking about what he would have for dinner before having back surgery the next morning should be given a tranquilizer.

It was given because it was written as an order on a chart by a physician who hadn't yet seen the patient, in anticipation of problems which did not occur. It's lousy medicine, but it's harmless—for the great majority of patients.

But not for recovering alcoholics. Because the body has difficulty telling Xanax from Jim Beam. That's why we use it in detox units. It's very effective at fooling the body into thinking it's still getting the alcohol it craves.

The most irritating thing about this episode, in our view, was that it occurred in a room directly below our office in the addiction treatment center of the same hospital. And the medication was ordered by a physician who supposedly knew something about alcoholism.

Select a physician who knows something about alcoholism or drug dependency. Whenever you've got a medical problem, go see him first. Then, if you need to be referred, let him or her work with the other physicians you see, and monitor your case to make sure you're not getting worse or being treated in such a way as to provoke a relapse.

Where to find this physician? Try asking around at AA, or

contacting the American Medical Society on Alcoholism and Drug Dependence for members in your area.

2. Work On Your Attitude. Probably the principal obstacle to successful treatment where we're dealing with more than one illness is *resentment:* the feeling of anger at the fact that you're unfairly burdened with two problems rather than one.

Here's how we recommend handling it:

Join a support group for your disease, if one is available. Call your local hospital or related association for information.

Work AA's Twelve Steps for your other disease as well as for addiction. Do a First Step, in which you acknowledge your powerlessness to handle this disease on your own, and the extent to which the powerlessness makes your life unmanageable. Do a Second Step, in which you acknowledge the need for help beyond your own resources. Do a Third Step, where you make a decision to seek out and follow guidance. Do a Fourth Step, in which you examine your attitudes for signs of resentment and defense mechanisms. Do a Fifth Step, in which you share your attitudes with another human being. And so on and so forth. It is the absolutely best thing for your mental health.

3. Encourage the People Who Live With You to Also Get Help. The people you depend on—and when you have diseases, you come to understand the true meaning of the word *depend*— forget that they, too, have needs, and they tend to bury themselves in your problems, your needs. Eventually, it makes them resentful and a lot less fun to be around. Remind them that you can do a lot for yourself and that they should get some kind of advice on how to live with your disease—because they're living with it almost as much as you are. Don't let your family life be ruined by a disease, whether it's alcoholism, diabetes, heart disease, cancer, whatever.

We've included some books for family members living with other diseases in our Suggested Reading section.

A Final Note

If you are given an addictive medication in the course of treatment for a medical illness, make sure you take no medications following discharge from the hospital without consulting with a physician who specializes in addictive disease. If craving returns—and it sometimes does—you could require assistance in avoiding relapse.

THE EIGHTH TRAP:
PSYCHIATRIC ILLNESS

"In a lot of ways, I was in worse shape after I quit drugs. Everybody else in the program was talking about all the great things they were going to do. I was just trying to compose a good suicide note."

—Recovering addict, age 29

You can imagine the problems that arise when you suffer both from addiction and from a coexisting psychiatric disorder. In the first place, they're difficult to separate: addiction mimics the symptoms of a number of common psychiatric disorders. The mood swings and anxiety of withdrawal are hard to distinguish from those of the manic-depressive or phobic. Drug-induced psychosis resembles a schizophrenic episode. Cocaine produces the paranoia, weight loss, abnormal sleep patterns, and suicidal thinking that characterize depressive disorder.

For most of this century, psychiatrists assumed the psychiatric disorder was primary, with drinking and drugs merely a form of self-medication for its symptoms. Such reasoning led to the erroneous conclusion that the best treatment for addiction is to address a wide variety of emotional and psychological problems. In our experience, that's the *worst* approach you can take, because of four problems:

1. Alcohol and drugs interfere with psychological change.

The essence of therapy is self-awareness. Self-knowledge takes different forms—from the insights of psychoanalysis to the emotional catharsis of psychodrama—but it must be achieved. Trying to understand ourselves while actively addicted to alcohol and drugs is like trying to exercise without increasing your pulse. The body doesn't work that way.

2. Addiction distorts the way you think and feel.

We knew a psychiatrist who went on a cruise with an alcoholic former patient. One night, the alcoholic got drunk and revealed a number of secret traumas from his past. The psychiatrist was surprised. "I had no idea his childhood had been so painful," the psychiatrist informed his colleagues. "This explains why he drinks." A week later, he discovered his patient's confessions were the product of his drunken imagination and had no basis in fact.

3. Relapsers drop out of therapy.

If an alcoholic can't stay sober, it's only a matter of time until he terminates treatment. Anything that increases his level of anxiety—such as therapy—will bring on another episode of drinking or drug use.

4. Addiction isn't the result of underlying psychological problems.

This of course is the root misconception of psychodynamic therapy. Alcoholism and drug dependency, rather than being handmaidens to mental illness, represent a distinct disease, with its own etiology, course, and prognosis. They may coexist in the same patient, but they don't cause one another.

If you find this difficult to grasp, try the following scenario. Suppose you possessed a radical new surgical procedure called a "personality transplant." You could take a cocaine addict, for example, and reverse his psychological makeup to its polar opposite. If he's introverted, you can make him outgoing. If his self-esteem is too low, feel free to boost it a hundredfold. If you find him immature, inject a sense of responsibility and social conscience.

Finished? He's a completely changed person. Now, let's reintroduce him to crack cocaine. We'll provide an abundant supply, a safe environment in which to use it, and a motive for experimentation. Then we'll go away for a year. When we come back, what do you think we'll find? Our guess is that he'll be right back where he started—low self-esteem and all.

Not that such an experiment will ever be performed: there are no therapies capable of making a fundamental change in someone's personality. Even an experience as far-reaching as recovery leaves your underlying personality structure virtually untouched. If you were terribly introverted as a child and grew worse as an alcoholic adult, you can't reasonably expect sobriety to turn you into a social butterfly. It's like the old joke where the patient asks his surgeon if he'll be able to play the piano after the operation. "I don't see why not," the doctor says encouragingly. "That's terrific," the patient responds. "I never could before."

Addictive disease and psychiatric illness qualify as a true *dual diagnosis*. Each disorder requires treatment, and the treatment of one invariably affects the treatment of the other. If you address psychiatric problems while ignoring addiction, progress will be slow or nonexistent. If you attempt to stay sober despite an untreated mental illness, the result will often be relapse.

ATTITUDE CHECK #8: PSYCHIATRIC PROBLEMS

Let's begin with a simple inventory of your attitudes and beliefs about your emotional state. *It is not to be used as an assessment tool for psychiatric problems.* Rather, its purpose is to help you identify some concerns that might require attention during the course of recovery.

Complete the following questionnaire, answering yes or no to the following statements:

1. I feel that I have had emotional problems since I was a child.
2. At some point in the past I gave up all drugs and alcohol for several months and still felt very depressed.
3. I have always been afraid of going crazy.
4. There is a history of mental illness in my family.
5. My biggest fear about sobriety is having to cope with depression and other negative feelings.
6. I began using alcohol (drugs) in response to severe anxiety or feelings of panic.
7. I have experienced severe mood swings during periods of sobriety.
8. I was a hyperactive child.
9. I sometimes have great difficulty controlling my emotions, even when sober.
10. I have been treated in the past for psychiatric problems.
11. I have been on psychiatric medications such as antidepressants or tranquilizers in the past.
12. I regard myself as an unusually fearful person.
13. Sometimes I experience anxiety to the point where I can't function.
14. I often find it difficult to motivate myself to perform my daily tasks, even when sober.

15. I go through periods where life seems meaningless to me.
16. At times I have thought about taking my own life.
17. Sometimes I get so angry I feel like hurting someone.
18. I have made a suicide attempt in the past.
19. I have been violent with others in the past.
20. In the past I have been told by a psychiatrist or other mental health professional that I suffer from a psychological problem.

Look at the box below for an interpretation of the results.

If you answered "yes" to less than three of the questions your chance of relapse is low. If you answered "yes" to between four and six of the questions your chance of relapse is moderate and you should continue to learn, and be aware of, the pitfalls of recovery. If you answered "yes" to between seven and ten of the questions you are at high risk for relapse and should pay particular attention to this trap. If you answered "yes" to eleven or more of the questions you are in a relapse "red zone" and need to seek and follow good advice immediately.

HOW THE TRAP CLOSES

Normally, this trap begins with the addict or alcoholic's struggles to deal with symptoms of a coexisting psychiatric disorder: recurrent depression, anxiety, mood swing, mania. Instead of seeking adequate treatment or following appropriate directions, the addict branches off into the following line of reasoning, which leads back to alcohol and drugs.

The first decision: The recovering person, afflicted with a psychiatric symptom, makes an error in judgment that pulls him away from effective treatment. Examples: he misidentifies the symptom as something else; he makes the mistake of assuming it will go away by itself; he decides to conceal it from other people.

Resulting behavior: He avoids seeking assessment and help from a qualified physician. Or, if he does obtain good advice, he fails to follow directions.

The second decision: As symptoms worsen, he begins to obsess about finding something to relieve them.

Resulting behavior: Search for temporary relief becomes uppermost in his mind—while larger issues of recovery fade in importance.

The third decision: Decides to reject alternatives to alcohol and addictive drugs. If offered, may claim that psychotropic medications such as antidepressants are dangerous, unreliable, or inadequate.

Resulting behavior: Returns to alcohol or other drugs. Relapse.

The fourth decision: Discovering that these substances provide some temporary relief, he increases consumption. If involved in recovery program or Twelve Step group, he will probably hide this from others.

Resulting behavior: Limits involvement in treatment or AA, or drops out entirely. Makes excuses for ignoring recovery; emphasizes debilitating effects of depression, anxiety, et cetera.

The fifth decision: In response to growing craving, increases dose of alcohol or drugs. Blames this on escalating anxiety or deepening depression. "I need more," he tells himself, "because I'm getting worse."

Resulting behavior: Incapacitating binge; toxicity; overdose.

RED FLAGS

If you find these phrases and others like them creeping into your thinking or conversation, you need to seek counsel from a professional or sponsor.

1. "I feel like I need help, but I can't go to a psychiatrist. People will think I'm crazy."
2. "I can't go to a psychiatrist. What if they want to put me on drugs or give me shock treatment?"
3. "I'm just under a lot of stress. You'd feel the same way if you had my problems."
4. "If anyone ever found out I saw a shrink, it would ruin my career."
5. "So I'm a little depressed? Everybody gets depressed."
6. "They're all trying to make me doubt myself."
7. "You're the one who's crazy, not me."

RELAPSE IN ACTION

The Odd Case of Irving Thannett

Now let's look at an example of someone trying to stay sober in the face of an untreated mental illness. Because this is a complex trap, we'll use a longer example. Note that the protagonist fails to recognize the presence of a mental illness until it is fairly advanced. This makes relapse virtually inevitable. Note also how he resists the advice of those around him: his family, friends, physician. Sound familiar?

Irving Thannett was one of the biggest producers in Hollywood and a chronic alcoholic. It took a medical emergency to finally deposit Irving Thannet in a hospital for alcoholism. The doctor advised him to eliminate alcohol and cut back on his seventy-hour-per-week schedule.

"You can't win an Oscar from bed, Doctor," Irving objected.

"You can't win one from a coffin, either, Mr. Thannett."

Properly intimidated, Irving sought the advice of an expensive Beverly Hills psychiatrist. Frankly, the prospect of sobriety terrified him. He feared he'd never relax or sleep again.

His fears were unwarranted. Quitting drinking seemed to release a flood of new energy. Some of his cynicism about the film industry—he liked to refer to it as "the place where morons hire psychotics to entertain the merely stupid"—began to wane. He found himself happier than he had ever been.

He decided to quit therapy. "I don't like to spend more than a few months on a project, Doctor."

The psychiatrist smiled patiently. "This isn't a movie, Mr. Thannett."

But that's exactly how Irving saw his life. It frustrated him that others didn't appreciate the importance of his role. After all, he was responsible for important films with budgets in the tens of millions, for the livelihood of hundreds of people, to say nothing of the millions, the *tens* of millions, who would eventually see his films in the theaters and on television and videotape, and who relied on him to bring a little light to their drab, difficult lives.

Irving stuck with therapy but quit AA. Soon afterward, he resumed drinking. There was no special reason. He simply couldn't remember why he had given up alcohol. He decided to keep this from his wife and the psychiatrist. After a while, the doctor started making funny noises about Irving's behavior.

"Your wife called me last week. After the session." The doctor shifted in his seat. "She's concerned about you. She thinks you're not getting enough rest."

"She worries. You know women."

"Still, you do seem pressured. Just an observation."

"Well, I don't think you can put anything you hear from your shrink in the category of 'just an observation,' " Irving said irritably. "You never once indicated anything was wrong, and now out of the blue you accuse me of being *pressured* . . ."

"It isn't an accusation. Why do you respond so strongly?"

Irving found himself getting really angry. "Because you're saying I'm in over my head, aren't you? That I can't take the pressure. See, this is the kind of thing," he went on, "that makes me *crazy*. I do the best I can under difficult circumstances, and get absolutely no support from anyone, if you get my drift."

Irving left the office in a fury. He couldn't remember being that angry in his entire life. Everything welled up inside him like lava overflowing a volcano. When he got home from the studio that night—around one A.M.—he woke his wife up and told her he wanted to have a little talk. He made sure to smile, to show her he was being completely rational.

"My darling, did you by chance call Dr. Epstein last week after my session?"

"Yes, I did, but—"

"Did you or did you not tell him that you were worried about me?"

"Of course, but—"

"Did you or did you not imply that I was overinvolved in my work, taking on more than I could handle?"

"Yes, but that's how I feel—"

"How *you* feel!" Irving thundered. "What about how I

feel! Having my psychiatrist throw that into my face! And don't tell me you haven't been spreading that rumor all over town!"

"I haven't, Irving—what's wrong with you?"

"What's wrong with *me!*" Irving yelled at the top of his lungs. "What's wrong with *me?* Nothing is wrong with me. Do you know what that could do to my career, if it got out that my own family thought I couldn't handle pressure?"

"Irving, please, you're frightening me . . ."

"I'll do more than that if you ever go behind my back again . . . I'll . . . I'll . . ." He turned and walked out of the room. Doris rushed after him, put a hand on his shoulder.

Irving whirled and punched her in the mouth. She dropped to the floor like a stone.

Two days later, Irving and Doris sat in Dr. Epstein's office. Doris had a bandage over the lower portion of her face. Irving hadn't bothered to shave.

"Mr. Thannett," the doctor said, "I want to try a medication. Lithium. It's something we use to level out mood swings."

Irving tried to object. Somehow, he was certain what these people were trying to do to him was wrong. But he couldn't seem to articulate that. He felt like he was walking around under a blanket.

"Whatever you think is right," he said. So Irving took the medication over the next few months. Everyone agreed he was doing a lot better. Everyone, that is, except Irving.

"I don't like feeling this *level* all the time," he told his doctor. "I miss getting really excited about an idea and staying up all night just to get everything down on a sheet of paper. Sure, ninety percent of the time it didn't work out, but I liked it anyway. I miss it."

"Do you miss the depressions, too?" asked the psychiatrist.

"No," Irving admitted. "I don't. When I was really down, I wouldn't drink at all—that would make it worse. Booze was for when I was really up, working on a film, going all the time. It helped me concentrate."

In fact, Irving had been thinking that if alcohol had worked once, it should work again. After all, he had gained a great deal of insight into himself. That's what psychotherapy was for, wasn't it? And there was always the Lithium. He could use the medication to counteract any adverse effects of the alcohol.

Of course, there was the warning label about mixing the pills with alcohol. But he wasn't going to dissolve the goddamn pill in vodka, for Christ's sake. He was just going to *alternate* them occasionally.

Irving developed a plan of his own. He would take the Lithium as prescribed. He would continue having his blood levels checked, to make sure he was in good shape. And he would drink six ounces of vodka every day. Two at 2 P.M., in his office. Two more ounces at 6 P.M., right before dinner, in his workshop in the basement. And the last two by himself, in the den after his wife went to bed.

As far as Irving was concerned, the experiment was a smashing success. Oh, sure, he frequently had to extend his limit—circumstances intervened to make strict control impossible—but all in all, he felt as good as ever.

After three months, Doris sued him for divorce.

"I can't prove it, Irving," she said as she packed his things for transport to his new apartment, "but you're drinking again. I just know it. Your moods are awful. I'm almost fifty years old, and I am entitled to half your money, and I do not have to put up with this."

So Irving left, moving into a little apartment that cost him over $1500 a month. With nothing to interfere, his drinking escalated. Soon, he was drinking over a fifth of vodka every twenty-four hours, and had foregone the Lithium completely.

Irving might have drunk himself to death had his pancreas not intervened. Once again, he found himself in the hospital.

Worst of all, he was under the care of the same internist who had warned him on his first visit.

"Back again, Mr. Thannett?" the doctor said. "Didn't follow my instructions?"

"I suppose I deserve this," Irving said. "But you have to admit, life according to your instructions seems pretty boring."

The doctor smiled. "My directions are supposed to save your life, not entertain you, Mr. Thannett," he said. "If you're looking for amusement, I suggest you try a movie."

HOW TO AVOID THIS TRAP

The first obstacle to dealing with a coexisting mental disorder is recognizing it.

Why People Deny Psychiatric Illness

Like alcoholism, psychiatric disease often goes unidentified. In fact, people frequently neglect treatment until the disturbance has become fairly advanced. It may require a crisis of one sort or another—a depression that won't go away, an episode of mania, a suicide attempt—to motivate treatment. If that sounds like what happens with addictive disease, it is. And mental patients fall into a pattern of denial for essentially the same reasons:

1. It's stigmatized. Like alcoholics and addicts, the victim of a mental illness believes that he or she is somehow "less okay" in the eyes of others than the diabetic or the heart patient. Unfortunately, there's plenty of evidence for this belief: recall that a candidate for Vice President of the United States was forced to withdraw when it was discovered he had a history of depression.

2. Most people regard mental illness as untreatable. This is fiction. Good treatments exist for most common psychiatric disorders, and new, more effective treatments are developed every year. We may not be able to effect a cure, but we can at least relieve many of the most bothersome symptoms.

3. *The signs of mental illness may come and go.* Like the problems associated with drinking and drug use, symptoms of depression or other disorders are frequently intermittent. When they diminish, people tell themselves they probably won't come back. When they do, they're a little worse.

4. *Defense mechanisms interfere with perception.* It's scary to think that you may have emotional problems. This tempts people to deny, rationalize, externalize, and minimize various symptoms. Some examples:

Denial (inability to recognize an illness in spite of numerous signs): "I don't know what you're talking about—I haven't been depressed."

Rationalization (making excuses for symptoms): "I know I haven't been out of the house in weeks, but I just don't *want* to leave. If I felt like going out, I would. But I don't. I just need a lot of time to myself, that's all."

Externalizing (blaming behavior on outside forces or circumstances): "If you were married to you, you'd cry all the time, too."

Minimizing (making symptoms seem unimportant): "I just don't see what you're so upset about. Okay, I lost my temper a few times. Everybody does. What's the big deal?"

The second obstacle is the longstanding belief that alcohol and drugs "help" when you're depressed.

The Myth of Self-Medication for Depression

In our culture, it's generally assumed that people who are depressed can obtain the most effective and immediate relief for their psychic discomfort through alcohol or drugs. Unfortunately, for many of us, it simply isn't true.

Imagine you're an alcoholic or addict. You're experiencing an episode of depression. You have no energy, motivation, interest in life. Everything looks hopeless. You hit on a remedy: getting drunk. *That will help,* you convince yourself. *Take my mind off my problems.*

But temporarily distracting yourself from your troubles is not the same thing as actually relieving your depression. Ask yourself: Will consuming enormous doses of a major central nervous system depressant improve your mood? Of course not. It will make it worse. In fact, taken in combination it will offset the benefits of any legitimate antidepressant medication.

Okay, you think irritably, *if I can't have alcohol, I'll do a little coke. I* know *that jacks me up.*

Sorry. Sure, you'll be happy for a little while. But what happens when the stimulant wears off? Your brain experiences a rebound depression. And the longer you've been using stimulants, the more persistent and painful this depression becomes.

Suppose you suffer from panic attacks. Every so often you find yourself in the grip of crippling anxiety: your heart racing, your stomach tight, as though under attack from an unknown enemy. You know a drink or a sedative will relieve it. But if you take them on a regular basis, you'll find that each time you use them they're a bit less effective than before. And when they wear off, you're sometimes stuck with a rebound anxiety that is even harder to get rid of than the original panic. Once again, you've discovered you can't successfully apply a short-term solution to your chronic problem.

Notice how in each case, your effort to alleviate the symptoms of the moment contributes to future distress. The sad truth: it's virtually impossible to successfully remedy the symptoms of depression by forcing your brain to contend with a whole new set of toxins. No matter how bad your anxiety or depression, self-medicating can probably make it worse.

This is yet another area where the addict's thinking may include some very strange paradoxes. An alcoholic who thinks nothing of knocking himself senseless with a fifth of vodka will stubbornly object to an antidepressant because it makes him drowsy. "But, Mr. Jones," argues his psychiatrist, "you've been drinking a bottle of whiskey every night before you go to bed." No matter; the alcoholic defends the toxin and rejects the medication.

What Is a Psychiatric Disorder?

When we talk about mental illness, we're not referring to the kind of psychological problems experienced by most human beings, including recovering addicts: conflicts with loved ones, feelings of guilt, sadness, remorse, resentment, anger, and so on. As painful as these may seem, they're essentially harmless—simply a by-product of being human. Instead, we're talking about a set of disorders that if untreated can come to dominate the life of the alcoholic or addict and make relapse virtually unavoidable. These fall into four broad categories: *mood* and *affective disorders, anxiety disorders, schizophrenia,* and *personality disorders.* We'll pay special attention to mood and anxiety disorders.

One of the continuing problems in psychiatry is the lack of recognized medical tests to identify common illnesses. As a result, the psychiatrist has to rely on the report of the patient (and family) as well as what can be observed by examination.

Mood and Affective Disorders

Mood is a continuing emotional state. Affect is its expression. Thus we *experience* mood and *exhibit* affect. Disorders in this area can be divided into several broad types. Let's begin with a look at depressive disorders.

Am I Depressed? If you've been alcohol- and drug-free for a period of at least three to six months and are still persistently depressed, answer the following questions with a simple True or False.

1. Since I quit drugs and alcohol I have experienced a significant change in my appetite, which has led to an unwanted gain or loss of weight.
2. Since getting sober I have been sleeping a great deal more (or less) than I want to.
3. People tell me that it looks like I'm not taking good care of myself.
4. I frequently find myself feeling very agitated.
5. I am constantly tired.
6. I don't seem to have much desire for sex.
7. I become tearful or depressed very easily.
8. I can't seem to concentrate on what I'm doing.
9. I sometimes think about killing myself.
10. I can't seem to get interested in anything.

Interpreting Your Responses. There are a number of different causes for the symptoms listed above. Some are medical, some psychiatric, and some are simply the result of physiology that isn't recovering from drug use as quickly as you would like. But if you answered True to three or more of the above, you may want to consult a physician or psychiatrist for evaluation.

Here are some of the disorders that a psychiatrist would look for:

Major depressive disorder is marked by a persistent feeling of sadness, irritability, or depression accompanied by loss of interest in usual activities. Its onset may be gradual or sudden. Some patients are diagnosed as depressive after only two to four weeks of unrelieved symptoms, which include:

1. change in appetite (with resulting increase or decrease in weight)
2. disturbed sleep patterns (too much or too little)
3. neglect of personal hygiene
4. agitation (restlessness, pacing) or retardation (sluggishness)
5. loss of interest in sex
6. fatigue, loss of energy
7. low self-worth, excessive guilt or remorse, desire to punish oneself
8. decreased concentration
9. preoccupation with death
10. suicidal thoughts, wishes, or behavior

Dysthymic disorder is yet another type of depression that differs from major depression symptoms in that its occurrences are generally confined to certain periods, which are interspersed with periods of apparently normal mood and functioning.

Bipolar disorder, once known as manic-depressive illness, is the third principal type. It's the most likely to be linked with excessive consumption of alcohol (this is what's wrong with Irving Thannett).

Mania refers to a dramatic change in mood, characterized by a euphoric sense of well-being, grandiosity, erratic or irrational behavior, and irritability (especially at the hint of setting limits on this behavior). During the manic phase, we may see:

1. hyperactivity or unusual restlessness, usually disorganized and without logical purpose, and perhaps quite bizarre (such as collecting possessions from other people, hoarding objects for no reason, flitting from activity to activity without reason)
2. pressured speech that may be difficult to follow and unrelated to the topic of conversation

3. flight of ideas, with rapid shifts between topics and apparent inability to focus on an issue or task
4. sleep disruption, including staying up for days at a time
5. involvement in activities that carry painful consequences (credit card overruns, buying sprees, sexual entanglements or affairs, drug or alcohol binges, reckless driving, unwise investments, et cetera) with no apparent recognition of potential risks

Manic episodes are frequently followed by painful depression where suicidal thoughts are not uncommon. Unless alcoholism is also present, drinking is largely confined to the manic phase, with alcohol providing the same calming effect to the manic's irritated nervous system as it does to that of a cocaine or amphetamine addict. Contrary to popular belief, bipolar patients drink little or not at all when in the grip of depression—alcohol deepens their melancholy.

Looking at the symptoms described above, we can see how alcoholism and drug addiction mimic these syndromes beautifully. So do hypothyroidism and a dozen other medical conditions. And until alcohol and drug use are eliminated for a period of several months and a thorough medical examination is completed, it's virtually impossible to reliably diagnose the presence of a coexisting depressive disorders. Many psychiatrists will refrain from making a final diagnosis of mood disorder for a year following the cessation of drinking or drug use. They'll treat the symptoms while reserving judgment about the cause.

Anxiety Disorders

Anxiety is a disturbance of the fight-or-flight mechanism. Our normal physiological warning system causes us to respond to danger with a rush of adrenaline, increase in heart and respiratory rate, and tensing of the muscles. When in the grip of fight-or-flight, we stop whatever we're doing—eating, working, resting—and prepare to respond to a perceived threat. But some of us experience fight-or-flight in the absence of danger. That's called a *panic attack*. Its victims face a dilemma: tolerate the anxiety or avoid any situation that might conceivably bring on an attack. This leads to two predictable outcomes: the *anxiety state,* where the victim suffers from chronic feelings of dread, and the *phobic disorder.*

A phobic disorder is marked by avoidance of an object or activity to the point where it interferes with the ability to function normally. Suppose you go to the supermarket one day and find that, without warning, you are overcome with crippling fear that renders you incapable of making a decision or carrying through your intentions. It passes, but you are terrified it will occur again, perhaps in a situation where you are unable to protect yourself. So you decide to avoid the circumstances that you associate with the panic attack. Some people decide to avoid the outside world altogether. This is known as *agoraphobia,* and is of course the most debilitating of the phobias. There are lesser phobias that center on aversion to specific things: tunnels, bridges, elevators, airplanes, trucks and vans, small spaces, windowless rooms, even certain food and drink.

Agoraphobia is especially common among women. There are many cases of otherwise quite competent females who remain housebound for years, using the telephone, their husbands, and their children and other "enablers" as their only contact with the outside world. Not surprisingly, there is a fairly high incidence of alcohol and tranquilizer use. If the phobic behavior persists despite prolonged sobriety, however, then it should be regarded as an independent disorder and treated accordingly.

Other disorders related to anxiety include:

Obsessive compulsive disorder (OCD), which features persistent intrusive thoughts about unpleasant or fear-provoking images or situations (obsession) coupled with repetitive activities believed to prevent some future catastrophe. Obsessions usually have to do with threats to personal safety: accidents, attack, disease or germs, contamination. Accordingly, compulsions often center around cleanliness, personal security, and avoidance of danger.

Panic Disorder, which is characterized by panic attacks featuring shortness of breath, heart palpitations or racing pulse, dizziness, shaking, sweating, and fears of insanity or death. Typically, such episodes are less than ten minutes long and go away by themselves. Because these symptoms (like depression) are mimicked by a variety of medical conditions as well as by alcohol and drug withdrawal and toxicity, a complete medical evaluation is of paramount importance.

Generalized Anxiety Disorder, which is marked by persistent symptoms (for a month or more) resembling those of panic disorder but perhaps less severe.

Like depression, anxiety disorders are very difficult to separate from the emotional augmentation (see page 24) that dominates early recovery. The fact that a recovering alcoholic may experience panic attacks and symptoms of depression during the first months of sobriety is not a very reliable indicator of coexisting psychiatric illness. In many instances, these symptoms will abate with time.

WHAT TO DO IF YOU THINK YOU MAY SUFFER FROM A PSYCHIATRIC DISORDER

Step One: Select a professional who knows something about addictive disease.

This isn't as easy as it sounds. Many psychiatrists believe they know a great deal more about addiction than they actually do. That also holds true for psychologists, psychiatric social workers, therapists, pastoral counselors, and helping professionals in general. There are three reasons for this:

1. *Many mental-health training programs are woefully inadequate in addictions training.* The most we can say is that they're better than they were twenty years ago. There are exceptions, but by our standards, the typical clinician completes his training largely unprepared to deal with addicted or alcoholic patients. He learns from experience.

2. *Many psychotherapists treat addiction as a result of underlying psychological problems.* This is left over from the phenomenal popularity of the psychodynamic model (see page 51) within the helping professions. It virtually ensures a high relapse rate.

3. *Many psychiatrists misuse medication with a recovering addict or alcoholic.* Like other physicians, they underestimate the influence of addictive disease on the addict's response to a wide variety of drugs. As a result, they may overuse medications, or, bedeviled by the addict's symptoms and complaints, pile one medicine on top of another in an attempt to offset unpleasant side effects.

One suggestion is to use a psychiatrist associated with an addiction treatment program, or who is a member of the American Society for Addiction Medicine.

We must warn you that there are a number of psychiatrists working in addiction treatment who know little about addiction. One young psychiatrist approached us after a lecture to admit that his training was woefully inadequate and to express serious reservations about dealing with alcoholic patients in his private practice. Two weeks later he was hired as medical director of a large inpatient program in a nearby city. Guess that's called "on-the-job" training.

So you're going to have to learn to interview prospective therapists with a list of questions in hand to help you determine whether or not they have anything to offer you.

Here is a suggested list. After you describe both the psychological problem you are currently experiencing *and* your history of addictive disease (in some detail), make sure to ask the therapist for his views on the following:

1. The cause of alcoholism or drug dependency. From his answer, you should be able to figure out which model he subscribes to. Our advice, which you may feel free to ignore: don't see a therapist who operates from a traditional psychodynamic model.

2. How he feels about using medication with recovering addicts and alcoholics. Be sure and ask about the use of tranquilizers such as Xanax, Valium, and Librium, and his feelings about the dangers of cross-addiction.

3. What he regards as a reasonable length of time for you to remain in treatment for this particular problem. Don't expect a therapist to tell you when you're "ready" to terminate therapy. Ask.

4. What his success has been in treating other patients with similar symptoms who were also recovering addicts. Don't ask for a "success rate": you'll get a meaningless and probably inaccurate subjective impression. Try to get him to describe a case. Does it sound like the way you'd like to be treated?

Step Two: Have your condition evaluated by this mental health professional.

This normally includes an interview, possibly with some psychological and laboratory testing. The psychiatrist may also want to talk with your family; their perspective may provide some valuable information.

If you feel the psychiatrist's evaluation is incomplete or you disagree with his finding, get a second opinion from another psychiatrist with a background in addictions treatment.

Step Three: Do what the doctor tells you.

The only area where this is generally difficult concerns medication. Most recovering alcoholics are rightly suspicious of physicians and their assurances that medications are "harmless"; AA is full of stories of people who were burnt by well-meaning prescriptions. But that's why you took such care selecting a physician. If you're not going to place your trust in that psychiatrist, what's the point of paying for treatment?

If at any point you find yourself overcome with doubt, you can always get a second opinion. And if you really do have a coexisting psychiatric illness, it should respond to treatment.

One word of warning: there's a big difference between *trust* and *dependency*. Many people remain in therapy solely because they have become emotionally dependent on a therapist. There is no intrinsic value in paying a professional for the right to take up space in his office every week. In fact, it's lousy for your self-esteem. So remember to look for a "working" relationship, and to keep your sights on an identifiable result.

THE NINTH TRAP:
COMPLICATIONS OF NORMAL RECOVERY

"Can you tell me exactly how many days I
have to stay here before I'm completely
cured?"

—Detox patient

Given the nature of addictive disease, probably the most unreasonable expectation for the first months of recovery is that you will feel good. It would be terrific if, once you made up your mind to give up alcohol and drugs, your body immediately forgave you for everything you'd done to it and spontaneously restored itself to glowing good health. But the body doesn't work that way, and therefore recovery is an extended process—physiologically as well as psychologically.

After all, diabetics continue to have symptoms from time to time even when their illness is reasonably well controlled. Heart patients experience episodes of tachycardia or angina on the road to recovery. They, too, find such symptoms frightening, uncomfortable, inconvenient. But they learn to accept it, and they learn that worry only aggravates their condition. Giving up on treatment is simply a shortcut to an early grave.

Paradoxically, we expect a great deal more out of recovery from alcoholism and drug addiction than we do from other diseases. We ask the diabetic and the heart patient only to do whatever is necessary to feel better and to return to something like normal functioning. With cancer, we're happy simply to see the patient survive.

Addiction gets different treatment. Abstinence alone is not enough. We begin with the expectation that the alcoholic avoid relapse, forever. We demand he achieve new levels of productivity at work or school. We feel uneasy if he fails to develop healthy, stable, mutually fulfilling relationships. We insist that he avoid other human problems, such as gambling, overeating, or promiscuity. We demand the pursuit of spiritual enlightenment, commitment, and self-actualization. And if the addict should fail in these areas, we're actually *disappointed*—as though nonalcoholics routinely achieved such goals.

As unrealistic as these expectations may be, they often match those of the addict himself. You, too, may anticipate an uninterrupted journey to the state of being "weller than well." And if it doesn't happen—if you experience further problems

—your first inclination might be to say "to hell with it," dump the whole project, and get loaded.

If you do, you're in for a rough ride. Sobriety might not be the *easiest* choice, but for the addict, it's the only one.

ATTITUDE CHECK #9:
COMPLICATIONS OF RECOVERY

To determine how you might respond to unforeseen symptoms during recovery, answer yes or no to the following statements:

1. I have a real fear of not being able to sleep.
2. I am extremely worried about gaining weight now that I'm not drinking or using drugs.
3. I'm concerned about sexual problems such as impotence or not being able to reach orgasm.
4. I don't know what I would do if I were to have a panic attack.
5. I have a hard time not turning to drugs or alcohol when I don't feel good physically.
6. I've always had problems sleeping.
7. I feel anxious much of the time.
8. I feel I am the nervous type.
9. I am very afraid of having flashbacks.
10. I have a lot of painful headaches.
11. I am experiencing more colds and infections than I did before I got sober.
12. I'm worried about what I will do when I am in pain and can't have a drug.
13. I'm concerned about my problems with memory.
14. I'm having difficulty concentrating and it's interfering with my life.

Look at the box below for an interpretation of the results.

If you answered "yes" to one or two of the questions your chance of relapse is low. If you answered "yes" to three or four of the questions your chance of relapse is moderate and you should continue to learn and be aware of the pitfalls of recovery. If you answered "yes" to five or six of the questions you are at high risk for relapse and should pay particular attention to this trap. If you answered "yes" to seven or more of the questions you are in a relapse "red zone" and need to seek and follow good advice immediately.

HOW THE TRAP CLOSES

The first decision: The recovering person decides that something he or she is experiencing—sexual dysfunction, insomnia, headache, et cetera—is not going to go away, despite assurances to the contrary.

1. *Resulting behavior:* Begins to focus on this problem rather than on recovery from addiction.
2. *The second decision:* The addict decides to devote his time to seeking a solution for second problem.
3. *Resulting behavior:* Becomes increasingly distracted from treatment of addiction and anxious about outcome of second problem.
4. *The third decision:* Decides that the second disorder is so disturbing that it justifies a return to alcohol or drugs.
5. *Resulting behavior:* Relapse, often accompanying a crisis.

RED FLAGS

Listen for these sentiments in your conversation or thinking:

1. "Sometimes I feel worse than when I was drinking."
2. "Maybe I've got another disease, something that will kill me even if I stay sober."
3. "Why go to the doctor? They're quacks, just in it for the money. Besides, these things don't always show up on their tests."
4. "I was miserable when I was drunk, but at least I could sleep (function, have fun, have sex, feel relaxed, et cetera)."
5. "I can't go on like this, without sleep (fun, relaxation, etc.). It isn't worth it."
6. "Maybe I'm mentally ill. Maybe people like me *need* drugs."
7. "It's easy for you to talk about sobriety. You don't feel like I feel."

RELAPSE IN ACTION

Here's a story about a recovering addict struggling to handle one of the most anxiety-provoking of all difficulties: a problem with sexual performance.

Dale Majors and the Art of Love

Like most addicts, Dale Majors experienced some pretty lousy things as a result of drinking and drugging. For a long time, nothing bothered him enough to discourage drug use. Then something happened to his most precious possession. Dale Majors became impotent.

Well, not *entirely* impotent. That was the worst of it: sometimes Dale's sexual abilities were amazingly intact. He'd meet somebody in a bar, take her home, and go fifteen rounds like the reigning heavyweight champ. On other occasions—well, Dale didn't even like to think about it.

Through most of his career as a doper—the drinking and the grass, fooling around with heroin and speed and LSD and loveboat—sex never deserted him. At first, spells of impotence came and went. But then there were weeks on end where he couldn't get it up. He discussed it with the doctor on his last day in the rehab program.

"Let me tell you, Doc, if I thought I was gonna be like this forever, I'd blow my brains out."

"Now, hold on a minute. There's a good chance it will go away. So why don't we be a little patient before we start talking about killing ourselves?"

"Okay, but I mean it. I am not going to live the rest of my life without drugs *or* sex. It just wouldn't be worth it."

Dale spent a month in the treatment center, and everyone agreed that he improved greatly in just about every aspect of his behavior. Unfortunately, there was only one aspect that Dale himself was interested in. He complained about this repeatedly to the doctor.

The physician tried to reassure him. "Dale, I think you're being too impatient. It took you a long time to get to this point, didn't it?"

Dale was doubtful. "You keep saying that. But how long? When will I be myself again?"

"I don't know any more about your body's timetable than you do. The only thing I can say for sure is that if you stay off drugs, sooner or later things will work out. And if you go back to drugs, they'll just get worse."

His first night home, Dale decided to test his sexual prowess by bedding his girlfriend. At one time, when they'd first met, the chemistry between them had been strong enough to ensure they spent every free moment in bed. Later, Dale's problems had driven a wedge in their relationship. He felt it was time to set things right.

That same evening Dale took Susan to a candlelit dinner,

then to a movie. By the time they got home, she was interested in making love. She put on a sexy nightgown and they climbed into bed, kissing feverishly.

Twenty minutes later, Dale got dressed and went out to buy some cigarettes. He was thinking about shooting himself in the head.

The next evening, a miserable Dale related the episode to his aftercare counselor.

"It's something that happens to some people, and we don't know exactly why," the counselor said.

"Yeah, yeah, I heard all that. But it doesn't help much at a time like this. What am I supposed to do? Go without sex for the rest of my life?"

"There you go with that rest-of-my-life bit again. Your body is not a machine. It gets well at its own pace."

"One day at a time, eh? Well, today I'm impotent."

Several months passed. Dale had to admit he was improving. *I can get an erection now. I just can't keep it hard long enough.*

Of course, Dale's girlfriend wasn't sure what was going on, either. They'd been together for about three years, during which time he'd gone from fantastic to pathetic in bed. She knew about his previous escapades, and wondered if there wasn't something about her that turned him off. Some physical flaw, or deficit in charm. The more she wondered about this, the angrier she got at Dale. *If he really loved me,* she told herself, *he would ignore whatever is turning him off to me.* Her attitude became one of unspoken reproach.

Dale sensed her anger but assumed it was simply because she was sexually frustrated. This made him feel even more ashamed. At the same time, he thought she was wrong to expect so much when she knew he was coming off alcohol and drugs, trying to get his career going and his head together. She came to represent a series of demands he could not meet. Their relationship deteriorated. Eventually, Dale suggested they separate.

Susan had an alternate plan: that they seek counseling for their sexual problems.

The counseling bore mixed results. He and Susan didn't fight as much, but he wasn't sure that represented progress. His special feeling for Susan seemed to have disappeared.

He was glad that his sexual function had returned, though in his heart of hearts he doubted the therapy had much to do with it. After all, he reasoned, most of the improvement had occurred before he got into counseling. It could be that his body had simply completed its recovery.

But the therapist assured him that wasn't the case, that dealing with his emotions and his underlying personality problems had been the key. The more he thought about it, the more he wondered why he wasn't drinking. The therapist had said his primary problem was psychological, with the drugs just a way of putting a bandage on the pain. So AA no longer seemed necessary.

Eventually, he started drinking again.

One night he went out with some of his buddies—he and Susan had been fighting again of late, and he thought it would do them both some good to cool off for a while—and one of them happened to pull out some coke. Before he had a chance to consider what he was doing, he'd snorted half a dozen lines and sent somebody's younger brother out to score some crack.

A week later, he came home. He hadn't eaten or slept to speak of in over five days. Susan's car was gone. He tried his key in the lock; it didn't work.

He pulled open the screen door and found a note wedged above the knob. It was from Susan, of course. Here is what it said:

Dear Dale,
I changed the locks. Don't bother trying to get in. If you do, I'll go to court and get a restraining order. Your clothes are in trash bags in the garage. You can get the rest of your stuff later. Your boss called and said you were

fired. I am finished waiting for you. I don't know if I ever want to see you
again.
   You son of a bitch. You weren't that good in bed, anyway.

                                                        Susan

This was one problem Dale knew how to fix. He headed for the liquor store.

CO-DEPENDENT ROLE IN THIS TRAP

As the story reveals, the co-dependent's response can be crucial in determining whether or not certain problems lead to relapse. In this example, we have *two* co-dependents, both of whom approach the problem in exactly the wrong way.

Dale's girlfriend Susan takes his difficulty personally, as though it were somehow her fault. That's natural enough—nine out of ten women might fall into this trap—but she subsequently turns her concern into a resentment against Dale. If he really loved her, she reasons, he could ignore or forgive whatever flaw made her repulsive to him. Women like Susan usually hate some aspect of themselves—they see their bodies as too fat, too long, too short, et cetera—so this line of thinking finds fertile soil. It poisons her love for Dale, however, and he would have to be blind not to sense her hurt and disappointment. Dale, like most men, is less complex in his interpretation. He simply assumes she is angry because she is sexually unsatisfied. He responds to her anger with shame, guilt, and a sense of personal failure. That in turn further damages their relationship and makes the environment hostile to sexual expression. Once upon a time, Dale was unable to "perform" in bed; now, performing is all he can do. The romance is gone.

There's a second co-dependent here: Dale and Susan's therapist. In all fairness, by this time their relationship is nearly ended and counseling is really just a substitute for separation.

But as therapists sometimes do, she complicates the problem with unnecessary psychological interpretations that minimize the importance of his previous drug use and the normal process of physiological recovery. She unwittingly discredits his faith in recovery until he can no longer think of a reason to stay sober. By distracting him from the task of remaining sober, she paves the way for relapse that will result in the final disintegration of their relationship.

HOW TO DEAL WITH PROBLEMS OF RECOVERY

What can you expect? Let's take a look at some of the common problems that sometimes accompany the addict into sobriety.

Insomnia and Other Forms of Disrupted Sleep

The most common complaint of early recovery, insomnia often manifests itself as a broken or "fractured" sleep pattern. Frequent awakenings followed by difficulty returning to sleep interfere with the body's ability to achieve an adequate amount of rest. You spend the night in bed but wake in the morning with a feeling of fatigue.

The principal problem with sleep loss is that it appears to be cumulative. Suppose you wake up every few hours and can't get back to sleep for thirty minutes. Over the course of a night you lose a total of an hour and a half. That adds up to more than ten hours of missing sleep per week, or forty hours per month. There's no practical way to compensate for missing that much rest.

Theories abound as to the cause of insomnia in recovering addicts. One of the most popular concerns deficiencies in a brain hormone, serotonin, believed to be depleted by alcoholic drinking. Once a serotonin deficit is established, it is difficult to remedy through diet. That's the reason for the popularity of tryptophan supplements in addiction treatment programs in the early 1980s; tryptophan was thought to cause the brain to produce more serotonin. The contamination scare of 1989, however, effectively put an end to widespread use.

Mood Swings

Every recovering person experiences a certain amount of mood fluctuation during the first months of sobriety. It is probably the result of the body's efforts to resensitize itself to a drug-free state (see Chapter 4 on emotional augmentation). It isn't always possible to clearly differentiate the mood swings of normal recovery from those that represent a coexisting psychiatric illness. The simplest test: recovery-based symptoms improve with time. Psychiatric disorders persist or even worsen.

Residual Tremors

Tremors come in two types: those that are visible (usually hands that shake) and those that aren't (the "inner shakes" described so vividly by detox patients). Though these are most obvious during the initial few days after cessation of drinking, they often return for brief periods over the first months of sobriety. They're more irritating than harmful, but they often frighten the recovering person, who may have convinced himself that the physical portion of recovery was long past. Tremors go away by themselves.

Flashbacks

Particularly common among those who have used hallucinatory drugs, the flashback is simply a recurrence of certain symptoms associated with intoxication. Flashbacks seldom if ever include actual hallucinations. More often, the flashback experience consists of perceptual distortion (of light, sound, color, or shape) and a healthy dose of anxiety. With his heart pounding and his senses seemingly in an uproar, the addict normally responds to the flashback experience with panic. There's no need: flashbacks are usually short-lived, and the more intense the experience, the faster it ends.

Anxiety

Like emotional augmentation, occasional anxiety is a normal accompaniment to biophysical recovery. That's what makes it so difficult for the psychiatrist to diagnose the presence of a legitimate anxiety disorder. Anxiety related to recovery usually has the following features:

1. Anxiety episodes—usually fearfulness, rapid heartbeat, dizziness, and difficulty breathing—are short-lived rather than sustained.

2. In the early weeks of sobriety, it's usually *free-floating:* that is, not clearly related to a particular stress.

3. In later months, it's often the product of a *specific thinking process,* such as remorse about past misdeeds or worry over future problems. You can eliminate or reduce such episodes by recognizing and abandoning these thinking patterns. Consult the works of Albert Ellis (founder of Rational Emotive Therapy) for practical techniques.

Food Cravings and Rapid Weight Gain or Loss

Your body is in the process of shifting from a "fuel economy" based on alcohol or drugs to one based on food. This means you may not respond to certain foods as you have in the past. Some foods—particularly those high in sugar or fat content—may be treated more as drugs than as nutrients by your evolving physiology. You may discover that certain foods produce unusual fluctuations in mood or energy level, from sedation to agitation, fatigue to stimulation. One sign that the body may be using a food as a drug is the presence of persistent craving. Another is compulsion: difficulty stopping once you've started eating a certain food.

If you want to test your response to a given foodstuff, try this experiment:

Day One: Skip breakfast and instead eat as much as you want of the food in question. Don't eat anything else for the rest of the morning. At one-hour intervals, take note of the way you feel. Are you unusually tired, energetic, anxious, sick to your stomach, et cetera? If so, tape your list to the refrigerator door. Eat normally the remainder of the day.

Day Two: Eat a normal breakfast and then take only liquids until lunch. Instead of lunch, eat as much as you want of the one foodstuff you're investigating. For the remainder of the afternoon, take only water or decaffeinated tea. At five P.M., do another "systems check" on your body. Note any unusual feelings and add them to the previous day's list.

Day Three: Eat normally until after lunch. Take in only water or decaffeinated tea for the rest of the afternoon. Instead of dinner, eat as much as you want of the food in question. Eat nothing after dinner except the tea and water. The next morning, describe how well (or how badly) you slept. Was there any change from what you usually experience?

You may notice that your body is using the food for a purpose other than nutrition. You might also discover that you're paying a price for this. Heavy doses of sugar-containing foods may induce temporary stimulation but also lead to a rebound depression not unlike that of cocaine. Foods high in fat content can provide temporary sedation, but often produce a hangover-like feeling of fatigue. If that is what happens during your experiment, try eliminating the food entirely from your diet. Substitute the dietary recommendations from one of the books listed in our Suggested Reading section.

Something to Avoid: The Just-Out-of-Detox Quick Weight Loss Diet

Want to make yourself absolutely miserable? Get all upset about the pounds you gained during the first months of recovery and decide to go on a crash diet. Here's what it will probably look like:

Breakfast: Strong coffee, probably garnished with cigarettes. Consume as fast as possible and get to work so as to take your mind off hunger.

Morning Break: Even stronger coffee, consumed even faster because you have to get away from the box of donuts somebody left on the counter.

Lunch: Two 16-oz. diet colas, chugalugged. Chase with coffee and cigarettes.

Afternoon break: Diet cola and antacid mints.

Dinner: Postpone as long as possible just in case you can get by without eating at all. About seven P.M., break down and head for the nearest fast-food restaurant. Consume two double hamburgers, large fries, a chocolate malt, and dessert, in less than fifteen minutes. Head for AA meeting.

At AA Meeting: Drink strong coffee, smoke cigarettes, and complain bitterly that you feel worse than when you were drinking.

Midnight: Since you can't sleep, go to all-night diner and have double portion of hot fudge brownie ice cream cake. Drink only diet soda to conserve calories. Smoke half a dozen cigarettes. Fall asleep just before dawn. Wake at seven A.M. vowing to give up food entirely.

We generally recommend that you not try to lose any large amount of weight in the first year of sobriety, unless your physician tells you it is currently threatening your health (as in the case of a diabetic, heart, or orthopedic patient). Before you go on a strict diet, consult your physician. An additional rule of thumb: get hold of a table listing *medically recommended* body weights for your age, sex, and height. Calculate the difference from your current weight. If you need to lose more than ten percent of your present weight, do so as part of a medically supervised weight-loss program. It's better for your health, and you'll increase your chances of keeping it off.

Forgetfulness

This is about as common as insomnia. Your memory can be divided into three distinct components, each of which can be tested:

Immediate Retention: The ability to recall information after a very brief interval.

An exercise: On a piece of paper, write out a four-digit number. Remember it. Put the paper in a drawer. Wait one minute. Reproduce the number on another sheet of paper.

Repeat the experiment with a five-digit number, then six digits, seven digits, and so on. You'll probably have some difficulty after seven or eight digits.

Short-term Memory: The ability to recall information after an intervening period of distraction.

A self-test: Write down what you had for breakfast this morning. Now write down what you had for dinner last night. Keep going back until you find you can't remember that particular meal. This process is often impaired in early recovery. It's why you should learn to take notes and record all appointments. Otherwise, you might forget them.

Long-term Recall: The ability to remember information that you haven't used for a long period.

An exercise: Remember an address or telephone number of a residence you haven't lived in for at least five years. This faculty is usually unaffected by alcohol and drug use.

Other Recovery Problems

Other problems that for many people are a normal adjunct to recovery include the following:

an increased incidence of food and fabric allergies

susceptibility to colds and infections

headaches, often related to menstrual cycles

aches, pains, and cramping

Most are harmless. If one worries you, follow these simple steps.

1. Don't Panic

A tendency toward panic may be your first inclination, especially during the emotionally augmented early months of recovery. Instead, take a longer view: you spent a long time disrupting your body's natural chemistry, and the symptoms you are experiencing are probably transient. One common error is to *interpret* these symptoms as a sign of another, more serious disease, thus justifying deep concern. Instead, try the following: make a list of the symptoms that bother you, noting their nature, duration, time of occurrence, and frequency. Turn to the section on normal symptoms of recovery, and read about the symptom if applicable. There are other good references as to the problems of recovery; check the Suggested Reading section in the back of the book.

2. Seek Advice From a Physician Who is Also Knowledgeable About Addiction

Here, as in our earlier examples, it's important to consult a physician who is familiar with the normal course of recovery from addictive disease. This physician can administer the appropriate tests to determine whether or not your symptoms are caused by something else.

3. Follow the Physician's Directions

If during your reading you come across a suggestion for alleviating your symptoms that your physician did not suggest, get his opinion as to its possible benefits and potential risks before putting it into effect. If your doctor advises you against something and you still feel you must try it, get a second opinion from another doctor first. Remember, for an addict, certain "treatments" are worse than the problem. Take care.

A Brief Exercise

Make a list of the things you're most afraid of: lost sleep, weight gain, sexual problems, perhaps simply feeling bad. Now imagine the result if you tried to remedy any or all of these with alcohol or drugs. Would they go away? Or would you ultimately cause them to worsen?

PROBLEMS OF ADDICTION

Most of the traps can be found wherever human beings struggle to change and to cope with any chronic disease. The final three, however, are closely tied to specific characteristics of addiction.

One danger for the addict is the temptation to switch from one drug to another, in the hope of finding the elusive "safe, nonaddictive" tranquilizer, stimulant, or painkiller. There are a lot of corpses littered along this road.

Another results from the addict's odd tendency to struggle against the treatment experience, even to the point of deliberate failure.

The last is a product of the remarkable changes that occur within the family system where alcoholism or drug dependency exists. These adaptations, unbeknownst to addict or family member, often encourage relapse rather than sobriety.

Read on.

THE TENTH TRAP: SWITCHING TO OTHER DRUGS

"I need something, for God's sake. Everybody needs *something*."

—Detox patient, age 21

We have a sneaking suspicion that the biggest single reason addicts relapse is that they try to substitute one drug for another, hoping that what happened with the first drug won't happen with the second.

Imagine you're in trouble with heroin. You've been trying to stop on your own, and you can't. Finally, you check into the hospital for detox, then enroll in an outpatient treatment program. *I'm finished with heroin,* you tell yourself. *It was a bad ride and I'm glad it's over.*

Shortly after entering the program, you sit down with a counselor to plan out your course of treatment. And that's where you get your first big surprise. The counselor asks you to pledge abstinence from all mood-altering drugs.

You: What? I came here to get off heroin.

COUNSELOR: This is a drug-free program.

You: Meaning I can't even have an occasional beer?

COUNSELOR: [nods] Nothing.

You: Look, I'll go along, but I can't honestly see why.

COUNSELOR: You'll learn. But if you show up dirty on the test, you'll have to leave the program. I want you to understand that in advance.

Later on, in group therapy, you bring up the issue for discussion.

You: Why is it they won't let us have a beer now and then?

FRANK [another patient]: Because they say you're cross-addicted. If you're hooked on one drug, you're hooked on all the rest.

You: I can't understand that. Suppose you've never even tried a drug? I've never had PCP. How could I be addicted to it?

FRANK: [shrugs] Beats me. But that's what they say. Ask somebody at the NA meeting.

Still later that evening, you take Frank's advice.

You: Say, they tell us that if you're hooked on one thing, you're hooked on everything. Is that true?

NA MEMBER: Sure. You have to give it all up. Total abstinence. If you use anything at all, it's a relapse, and you'll be back into dope before you know it.

You: Isn't that a cigarette in your hand? And a cup of coffee you're drinking?

NA MEMBER: Yeah, so what?

You: They told us in the program that nicotine and caffeine are drugs, and you can get addicted to them.

NA MEMBER: That's different.

Still later, you're lying in bed, waiting to fall asleep and thinking about the whole issue.

What I don't get is how you can be addicted to something you've never used. They must be making a lot of this up, just to scare us away from drugs . . . kind of like Prohibition, or something.

At the next group session, you seek out another member who seems as skeptical as yourself.

You: Say, what do you think about this idea that you can't even have a beer once in a while?

Bob: I think it's bullshit.

You: Yeah, so do I.

Bob: Let you in on a secret: I been havin' a couple beers after these groups. I figure they're not going to test me till the next meeting, right? And alcohol gets out of your system real fast. So where's the risk?

You: You don't think that's cheating?

Bob: Hell, no. I'm not doing heroin. I'm not doing anything illegal. I'm just relaxing. If these counselors can't deal with that, it's their problem.

This starts you thinking. *If Bob can get away with having a few beers, then why can't I? He's not falling back into drugs. These counselors are definitely feeding us a line.*

So you decide to try it yourself. One evening after group you stop off at a package store and buy a six-pack of Tallboys and a package of breath mints. You go off by yourself and drink a beer. You think you're taking your time, but before you know it the can is empty. As you crumple it up you're already thinking about the next one. You decide to have a second can and then a third. You pop a couple of mints. *I'd better get home,* you think anxiously. On the way, you pull over and throw the last three beers into a dumpster as a sign of your commitment to sobriety.

The next day you wake up feeling terrific. *Wow,* you say to yourself. *I knew it. Nothing happened.* To test your resolve, you decide to abstain for a week. *Just to make sure I don't really want the stuff—that I can take it or leave it. And that I won't crave heroin.*

The week passes slowly. You don't have any particular desire for heroin (at least any worse than usual), but you keep thinking about how good those beers felt on the way down, and how you probably could have treated yourself to a couple more without mishap. Finally, Friday comes, and the experiment is over. You drank and you stopped, with no help. The great cross-addiction myth is laid to rest. You're well on the road to recovery.

So that evening, after group—you remain quiet, not wanting to give away your little secret and bring everyone's wrath down on your head—you decide to stop off and buy another six-pack and have yourself a little party. After all, your family isn't expecting you home right away.

Twenty minutes later, you're sitting in your car drinking beer and thinking, *Wow, this is pretty good. But you know what, a little coke would really top it off:* . . .

Another twenty minutes passes. You're on the phone to your old connection, arranging to pick up some cocaine. You rifle through your wallet looking for the money-machine card, hoping there's enough in the checking account to cover your buy. All the "issues" that were so important a few days ago are forgotten. There's only one agenda in your head now. *As long as I'm copping,* you think, *I might as well pick up a little smack:* . . .

Two months later, broke, sick, homeless, and suicidal, you're admitted to detox again.

*   *   *

Before we analyze this series of events, let's take a look at some attitudes that might influence you to substitute one drug for another. Respond honestly; remember, this is just between you and your disease.

ATTITUDE CHECK #10: SWITCHING SUBSTANCES

We've divided the following inventory into two sections, based on your "primary drug": the drug or drugs that brought you into treatment. If you've been treated for different primary dependencies at different points in your life (say, you got off cocaine but later needed help for alcohol abuse), complete both sections. As always, answer yes or no to the following statements:

Section One: For Primary Alcoholics

1. I feel that I will have considerable difficulty coping with certain problems or moods without alcohol.
2. I don't feel comfortable in Twelve Step groups.
3. I believe that much of my drinking was in response to certain situations or problems in my life.
4. I have used marijuana without any problems in the past.
5. I've experimented with other drugs without experiencing a craving or desire to use them again.
6. I have used sedatives or sleeping pills in the past.
7. I never had a problem with sedatives or sleeping pills.
8. It bothers me to think that other people can drink and I'm forbidden from using anything at all.
9. I wonder how I will cope with (sleeplessness, headache, anxiety, depression, fatigue, worry) without resorting to alcohol, or some other drug.

10. My regular doctor has prescribed sedatives or sleeping medications for me in the past.

Section Two: For Primary Cocaine, Narcotic, and Other Drug Users

1. I used drugs for a long time before I got in trouble with them.
2. Even when my drug use was at its worst, I could smoke marijuana (or take a pain pill) without problems.
3. I don't consider myself an alcoholic.
4. I never used alcohol except in social situations or to offset the effect of cocaine or a narcotic.
5. I feel it will be very hard to cope with my moods and feelings without some kind of chemical.
6. I never had a problem with alcohol or sedatives.
7. I never had a problem with marijuana.
8. I never had a problem with pain pills.
9. It bothers me to think that other people can drink and I'm forbidden from using anything at all.
10. I wonder how I will cope with (sleeplessness, headache, anxiety, depression, fatigue, worry) without resorting to drugs.

Look at the box below for an interpretation of the results.

> If you answered "yes" to one or two of the questions your chance of relapse is low. If you answered "yes" to three or four of the questions your chance of relapse is moderate and you should continue to learn and be aware of the pitfalls of recovery. If you answered "yes" to five or six of the questions you are at high risk for relapse and should pay particular attention to this trap. If you answered "yes" to seven or more of the questions you are in a relapse "red zone" and need to seek and follow good advice immediately.

HOW THE TRAP CLOSES

This trap normally begins with two incorrect assumptions. First, that problems with one drug do not put you at risk for problems with another. Second, that using a mood-altering substance will not substantially undermine your ability to avoid a return to other drugs.

Let's review the thinking process.

The first decision: The relapser questions the need for total abstinence from all mood-changing chemicals.

Resulting behavior: Seeks alternatives to abstinence.

The second decision: The relapser, perhaps noticing that not all drugs (e.g., nicotine, caffeine) produce relapse to alcohol, cocaine, and the like, seeks evidence that general prohibition is unjustified.

Resulting behavior: Seeks out others who have experimented with drugs and questions them about their experience. Probably meets people who reinforce his belief that cheating is okay.

The third decision: Advances "comparing out" process, emphasizing in his thinking (and to others) the positive aspects of his experience with other drugs, and downplays the negative aspects.

Resulting behavior: Aligns self with those attempting to control use of alcohol or drugs.

The fourth decision: Loses identification with abstinent addicts.

Resulting behavior: Isolates self from recovering community.

The fifth decision: To experiment with controlled use of drug other than one that has brought him or her to treatment.

Resulting behavior: Begins to use a drug other than his primary drug.

The sixth decision: Normally, decides that success in using this drug is a signal to further test himself with more drug use.

Resulting behavior: Probably launches self-directed "behavior modification" program to prove that control has been regained.

The seventh decision: Interprets success at maintaining control as evidence that consumption of drug is safe.

Resulting behavior: Relaxes external controls; usually goes on a binge and returns to primary drug.

RED FLAGS

Watch for these and similar phrases in your thinking or conversation:

1. "Sure, cocaine is bad, but I never had any trouble with booze or grass."
2. "How can I be addicted to something I never even tried?"
3. "You mean if I have one beer, I couldn't stop and I would be an alcoholic forever?"
4. "I don't crave it . . . If I were going to relapse, wouldn't I have a craving?"
5. "I'll be honest with you: I had a drink (joint) a couple of weeks ago, and I didn't go on a binge or nothing. If what you said were true, I would not have been able to stop."

RELAPSE IN ACTION: YOU AND THE SUBSTITUTION MODEL

We've already illustrated the dynamics of this trap in our initial example. Now, we'll analyze it. Read it once again. Here are the six mental errors that led to a painful outcome:

Error One: You Focused All Your Attention on One Drug

It's natural enough—after all, most people don't come into treatment because they've lost control over every substance they've ever used. Most have a reservoir of "good" experiences with marijuana, alcohol, minor tranquilizers and painkillers. That makes it easy to "compare out" in this respect.

You may remember the term *comparing out* from the second trap. Comparing out occurs when you examine your history for problems you *don't* have rather than for those you do. It's a trademark of addictive defenses, and we've yet to meet an alcoholic who doesn't indulge in it. And one principal way to compare out is to focus entirely on your experience with one drug while ignoring any discussion of others.

For instance, while reading the above story, did you find yourself thinking, "This doesn't apply to me . . . I've never used heroin . . . I don't drink beer . . . Cocaine was my drug . . . Why don't they use examples you can relate to?" You've provided a perfect illustration of the comparing-out process.

Error Two: You're Not Given an Adequate Explanation of Why You Can't Use Marijuana (or other drugs of apparently "mild" effect)

This is the treatment program's fault. After all, it's the professional's job to educate the patient about the disease, and in this case they clearly didn't. Most treatment programs are strongly therapy-oriented—that is, they devote most of their time and attention to exploration of feelings and motives. But in this quest for insight, they often forget the obvious: the newly sober addict or alcoholic is largely ignorant about recovery.

Error Three: You Got Sidetracked by Your Question About Nicotine and Caffeine Use

Granted, it's a good question. Why don't nicotine and caffeine—both stimulants and addictive drugs—lead to relapse for alcoholics and cocaine addicts? It's relatively simple: the form in which you use them (generally, cigarettes and coffee) is too weak. For example, there's enough nicotine in the typical cigar to kill you. You lost the majority of it in the smoking process. If you extracted some of this nicotine and injected it, you'd get a rush not unlike a powerful amphetamine. If coke were your primary drug, you'd be out searching for crack in a matter of minutes.

Normal consumption of nicotine and caffeine, however, doesn't seem to awaken the craving for other drugs. But if you boost the dose by taking caffeine pills or consuming enormous amounts of coffee, you may find that your craving for drugs returns. Of course, most programs recommend you give up

caffeine and nicotine anyway, for reasons of physical and psychological health.

Error Four: You Find Yourself an Ally in Your Thinking

One common slogan within Twelve Step groups is "Stick with
the Winners." Many relapsers do exactly the opposite. They
seek out those whose ideas correspond to their own—setting up
a "support group" for failure.

Error Five: You're Fooled by Getting Away With Experiments

One of the problems with experimentation is that each successful outcome builds your confidence, perhaps unjustifiably. It's
like a heavyweight boxer who goes undefeated while fighting a
succession of easy matches. His success convinces him to step up
in class. As soon as he does, he gets knocked out.

Error Six: You Keep Your Experiments a Secret

You know that people will question your judgment, so you keep
your decisions to yourself. *What business is it of theirs?* you tell
yourself. *I'm taking care of things.* But when you get in trouble,
there's no one to turn to. In order to ask for help, you'd have to
admit you were lying all along.

CO-DEPENDENT ROLE IN THIS TRAP

Perhaps more often than in any other trap, the role of primary
enabler may fall to the physician.

For decades, physicians were taught that alcoholics drank
because they were depressed, under great psychological stress,
or inordinately anxious. To a doctor, bred to identify and allevi-

ate symptoms, this is like waving a red flag in front of a bull. Physicians and pharmaceutical companies rushed to develop new substitutes for alcohol. One after another, various barbiturates, narcotics, and benzodiazepines were introduced as safe, nonaddictive replacements, good for easing tension, relieving pain, inducing sleep, reducing depression. Each proved to be in some ways more dangerous for the alcoholic than the last.

In most cases, he or she simply returned to drinking. In others, a new addiction appeared, to the prescribed medication.

A good example is *methadone maintenance*. Here, the narcotics addict is given a daily dose of a powerful narcotic. The intent is twofold. First, the methadone will "block" the experience of euphoria. An addict who shoots heroin on top of a methadone dose should feel nothing. Second, the innate craving for narcotics will be satisfied. We know the addict will continue to show up at the clinic to obtain the methadone, because if he doesn't, he will become very sick. Theoretically, methadone maintenance makes it both impossible and unnecessary to continue the practice of injecting opiates. That in turn eliminates the need to steal to support a habit. Perhaps more importantly, it greatly reduces the risk of spreading HIV through needle sharing.

These two benefits alone justify methadone maintenance programs to legislators, social scientists, and the medical community. Unfortunately, many laypeople confuse maintenance with eliminating drug abuse. They're not the same thing at all. Many maintenance patients use a greater variety of drugs than when they were street heroin addicts—stimulants such as crack and ice; depressants such as alcohol, tranquilizers, other narcotics, and PCP. In some cases, they inject these drugs.

So maintenance must be viewed as a "drug-taking control strategy" rather than treatment. It's a spiritual cousin of the nineteenth-century experiments in which chronic, relapsing alcoholics were addicted to morphine.

HOW TO AVOID THIS TRAP

What's wrong with substituting one drug for another? Actually, two things. First, the drug itself is often cross-addictive. That's why you find it attractive. Second, even if not technically cross-addictive, it normally provokes relapse anyway.

How Cross-Addiction Works

Here's something to remember: Addiction to one drug is addiction to all drugs of the same general effect.

It's one of the most important concepts in addiction. If you don't learn it, you can't stay sober. Because sooner or later, you're going to be tempted to try a drug other than the one which landed you in treatment.

Suppose your primary substance has always been alcohol. Once your brain and liver have adapted to the point where you suffer from alcoholism, then those same adaptations will affect the way you respond to other drugs of similar effect—Valium, Xanax, and other benzodiazepine sedatives, for example; or barbiturates and nonbarbiturates like Quaalude and meprobamate. That's why these drugs are used in detoxification programs. The nervous system can't effectively differentiate them from vodka.

But drinking can impact your use of drugs less closely related to alcohol, as well. Alcohol is, pharmacologically speaking, a "dirty" substance. It acts in more than one way and at a remarkable number of locations in the brain. Instead of deriving its effect solely from its action at the synapse—as cocaine does—alcohol has an effect on the entire cell membrane, changing its conductivity to key substances. That's partly why alcohol acts both as a stimulant at low doses and as a depressant at higher doses, as well as (in some respects) a hypnotic, an anesthetic, even an hallucinogen. Thus alcohol might be said to be "more cross-addictive" than some other substances.

Athletes sometimes make this mistake. You'll read every once in a while about a famous athlete who has been arrested for cocaine use after completing a treatment program. In most cases, the drug use actually began with alcohol. Athletes, like most recovering addicts, are more than willing to acknowledge that cocaine was a problem, but often seem to feel that drinking beer is a birthright which cannot be renounced. So they continue to go out drinking with the boys until, one evening, the same thing happens to them that happened to you in our original example.

We often cite the story of the basketball player who was banished from the league after his third unsuccessful treatment. A story in a sports magazine described the confusion experienced by his teammates. "He was doing so well," was the general consensus. "We were just out drinking with him, talking about how well he was doing."

Another common "gateway drug" for relapse is marijuana. There are two reasons. First, many kids begin using grass even before they start drinking. It's easier to get. You don't need a fake ID; you can buy from a kid on the playground. So the addict usually possessed the required history of positive experiences with the drug. Secondly, marijuana hasn't brought about what the addict has identified as "problems," and doesn't produce obvious intoxication, so the addict has already decided it's harmless. And then one night, when he's smoked a little too much and is feeling kind of confused, an idea pops into his head: *I know what will make this feel better: . . .*

Exercises for Avoiding This Trap

Of course, there's only one reliable way: practicing abstinence.
And that's exactly what the addict is looking to avoid.

Most alcoholics learn about the need for abstinence through
failure. If they're lucky, they go through this learning process
before they ever reach treatment, and don't feel the need to do
further research, looking for the safe, nonaddictive drug. If they
still cling to the belief that somewhere there exists a safe,
nonaddictive substance, they will probably experience at least
one "slip" in their attempt to locate it. The good news: their
experience should teach them a lesson.

Brain Television

Turn on your brain TV. Picture the two control knobs; the one
on the left permits you to adjust the volume and the intensity of
the image on the screen, and the one on the right changes the
channel. Ready? Picture a situation in which you were under
some type of stress: you were angry or upset, frustrated or
deeply disappointed. Got it? Watch yourself in the situation for
a few seconds—just stay with the feeling.

Okay, now reach out and change the channel to a blank
screen. Finished? Now let still another image appear on the
screen, this time *another* situation in which you felt the same or
similar feelings (for most recovering people, this isn't difficult).
Watch it for a minute or so. Then reach out and change the
channel, so you're once again looking at a blank screen.

Now, reach out and switch back to the first scene of you
feeling stressed. Think about what a drug would do for you in
that situation. Experience that feeling for a moment—that
sense of relief. Then reach out and change the channel, to a
blank screen. Relax for a second. When you're done, turn off the
TV set.

You should now understand how this trap works, and where

the temptation to substitute one drug for another comes from. Now complete the following exercise.

History of Drug Use

Step One: Make a list of all the drugs you've ever used, and the general reason you used them (to get high, relax, relieve pain, et cetera). Rank them in order of importance in your history. Which ones were the most important to you? Which the least?

Step Two: Now, tell the story of your addiction, giving each drug a role. In other words, how did each drug drive you closer to treatment? For example:

"I started smoking marijuana when I was fifteen. Maybe if I hadn't, I wouldn't have had the confidence to try stronger drugs."

"I never used PCP, but I had a friend who did, and he didn't go crazy like they said he would. So I figured everything they said about drugs was a lie."

"I never was much of a drinker, but when I was coming down from cocaine I would use alcohol to level me out."

"I wouldn't have used illegal drugs, but I thought a tranquilizer or a pain pill was all right because it came from a doctor."

"I thought I was just nervous, but maybe I was really in withdrawal and the pills were to take the place of the alcohol."

Step Three: When finished, go over your revised history with a counselor or sponsor. Look critically at the way you see your drug use. Are there still places or situations where you feel substitution of "lesser" mood-altering drugs would be safe? Discuss this.

THE ELEVENTH TRAP:
RELAPSE BY INTENT

"What you do with your own body is *your*
business. Especially if it might kill you."

—Cocaine addict, age 33

"I think everybody needs to blow off steam
from time to time."

—Alcoholic, age 46

Some addicts and alcoholics relapse for the simplest reason of all: it was never their intention to remain sober.

A certain percentage acknowledge this openly. "I didn't want to quit," they insist. "It was somebody else's idea, and I just went along with it." Others admit it to themselves but conceal it from friends, family, and counselors. They do and say all the right things in treatment, then get loaded at the first opportunity. Still others—remember, addiction is characterized by *denial*—conceal their intentions even from themselves.

Hard to imagine? Here are three examples from our files. Each one will provide a key observation. Let's begin with an addict whose plan is all too obvious.

Case One: Izzy's Story

Izzy arrived in detox with all the trappings of a rock-and-roll star: two beautiful girlfriends, a harried manager, even two backup musicians so he could practice. After ten years of heroin, the thirty-four-year-old musician could easily pass for forty-five.

"What about a blood exchange?" Izzy asked the doctor during his admission physical. "Where they give you somebody else's blood. I think the Rolling Stones had one."

"I think simple detoxification will do the trick," the doctor replied.

Izzy spent the next three days in his room, emerging only for medications, sympathy, and bags of Hershey's Kisses. The fourth day he agreed to attend a group therapy meeting.

"I'm really glad to be here," he told the group. "It's been unbelievably difficult, but it's worth it."

"How you gonna stay off dope from now on?" asked another patient, somewhat in awe of Izzy's celebrity.

Izzy was puzzled. "I'm not gonna stay off dope. I like dope. The only bad thing about heroin is the expense, and I can afford it."

Now it was our turn to be confused. "So why are you here?"

"To get the high back, of course. See, after you been shooting awhile, you can't get off too well anymore. Outside of taking the edge off your sick, heroin don't do much. But after you detox, you get off real good again."

"You've done this before?" we asked.

"Twice a year," Izzy said. "Always before a tour. If I like this hospital, I'll put it on my preferred list."

"Don't the hospitals object?" we asked.

"I pay my bills." He grinned. "And I give 'em a big donation to the building fund."

Observation: With the exception of his financial resources, Izzy's reasoning is typical of many addicts. Treatment doesn't terminate drug use, it facilitates it.

Case Two: Cindy's Story

Here, the addict knows the truth but carefully conceals it from everyone else.

Cindy, a postal employee, was found intoxicated at work, and allowed herself to be referred into a psychiatric hospital as an alternative to being fired. Surprisingly, she was very compliant.

"I'm really glad to be here," she said. "I think it's a terrific opportunity to find out if I have a drinking problem." She was very active in group therapy. "This is terrific," she told her counselor. "I was so lucky to be able to come to a place like this." Cindy seemed to do beautifully on weekend passes with her family, and when the doctor finally discharged her, it was with a good prognosis.

Two months later, her husband came to see us. He told us the story of Cindy's treatment and that she'd been drunk since leaving the previous hospital.

"Looking back," he said, "I think she was sneaking drinks on those weekend passes."

"Didn't the psychiatrist pick up on any of this?" we asked.

"No. Cindy can fool people—she's done it to me a million times. I can tell you this: she never, not even for a minute, had any intention of staying off alcohol. She just wanted to save her job. Now that she's been through treatment, it doesn't matter how much trouble she gets in—they can't fire her for drinking. She's sick, see? It's all a big game to her."

Observation: This relapser often enters treatment with a hidden agenda—the desire to avoid a specific consequence of drinking or drug use. This is the motive behind the superficial compliance with the treatment program. As a matter of fact, the treatment staff is in the dark like everyone else.

Last, an example of an alcoholic who doesn't realize he plans his relapses.

Case Three: Boris's Story

Boris's contracting business had grown to the point where he could hardly keep up with its demands. He worked twelve hours a day, seven days a week. His wife and kids begged him to slow down. "You can't, in this business," Boris insisted. "The competition will kill you."

Boris was also a chronic alcoholic. Every eight or nine months—usually when his wife was out of town—he would go off on a binge. His wife would return home to find the house a wreck and Boris unconscious on the living-room couch. She'd call the family doctor, who would admit him to the local hospital. Three days later, Boris would go back to work.

Boris was very embarrassed by his "weakness." He never attended AA because of his busy schedule and the fear he might run into a customer. He did however take Antabuse to help him stay away from alcohol. After each episode, Boris swore to his family that it would never happen again.

Yet six to nine months later—as regular as clockwork—it did.

"What's going on here, Boris?" his doctor asked. "You seem to be doing well, and then boom! off you go again."

"I know, I know, I'm sorry to be such a bother."

"Doesn't this cause trouble for your business? And your family?"

Boris looked uncomfortable. "At least I can say I always take care of my responsibilities. I never drink when my wife or my children are around. I wouldn't want them to have to see that. And I hired a wonderful woman to manage my office and a young fellow to supervise the construction. So I can say no client is ever disappointed with our work—even if I'm, well, sick. They don't even know about it."

"If I didn't know better, I'd say you planned these things."

Boris looked surprised. "You shouldn't make jokes about this, Doctor. I try my best, but sometimes it isn't good enough. I'm only human."

Observation: Boris has arranged and adapted his lifestyle not to prevent but to *permit* periodic relapse.

*   *   *

Put the observations from these three cases together and you have three of the five trademarks of this peculiar trap.

Trademark one: Treatment becomes part of the *enabling* syndrome: the network of people (and sometimes institutions) that protects the addict from the consequences of drinking or drug use.

Trademark two: There's a hidden agenda, a goal that is important to the addict but has little to do with recovery itself. Some examples: keeping a job, avoiding a divorce, holding onto a driver's license, staying out of jail.

Trademark three: The relapser suffers few major consequences as the result of relapse. To make this possible, he or she needs a "safety net" for protection.

Trademark four: The relapses follow a fairly predictable timetable. In other words, relapse normally accompanies certain events. One alcoholic drank whenever her husband left town on a business trip. A professional athlete avoided cocaine during the playing season and binged after the final game. A school psychologist went on a drunk as soon as school let out.

Trademark five: The pattern seems "treatment-proof"— even through multiple hospitalizations or extended therapy.

As you might imagine, this trap provides the hidden foundation for many cases of *chronic relapse*—where years of treatment are punctuated by multiple relapse. This is the pattern that convinces the public that treatment is worthless, and gives both family and professionals an endless supply of headaches.

"Tell me the truth," a worried father begged. "Does my son relapse on purpose, or is he just deluded?"

When you're dealing with this peculiar trap, the answer to both questions is yes.

To grasp the unusual logic, we must remember that people give up alcohol and drugs for different reasons, some of which are better than others. When you enter treatment you're not necessarily looking to renounce drinking on a permanent basis.

Your primary focus is on reducing, eliminating, or avoiding certain *problems* associated with drug use. If it weren't for those problems, you probably wouldn't have come to treatment at all.

Of course, since the nature of addiction is to continue using the drug despite its adverse consequences, you may have allowed problems to reach a sort of *critical mass* before consenting to treatment. Prior to this point, you've probably worked overtime to keep your life together despite drinking or drug use. It's entirely possible that had you been able to figure out a way out of your current crisis—through borrowing money, getting a credit extension, pleading with the family, lying to your probation officer, hiring a sharper lawyer, going on the wagon for a while, conning some pills from your doctor—you would have jumped on it.

So the motivation that brought you to treatment isn't the same one that keeps you sober in the long term. That incentive comes from recovery itself. You begin to feel better, to understand more about your disease, to experience life without the cycle of intoxication and withdrawal. Sobriety reinforces itself.

But some people never experience these rewards. Their thinking when sober is hard to distinguish from the way they thought while in the grip of alcohol or drugs. Their sobriety remains of the "white knuckle" variety—perhaps dominated by obsession and compulsion, fear and resentment, isolation and disappointment. For such people, abstinence is a necessary but unpleasant interruption in drinking or drug use. Periods of sobriety are grim sentences to a personal prison. Binges are a form of holiday. Treatment is part of a larger effort toward "damage control."

ATTITUDE CHECK #11: RELAPSE BY INTENT

Let's see whether or not your attitudes reflect a tendency toward this trap. Answer yes or no to the following statements:

1. I believe that everyone needs to blow off steam from time to time, myself included.

2. I think most people would consider me a workaholic.

3. I'm a very dynamic person. When I do something, I tend to do it all the way.

4. I believe that you can do whatever you want if you put your mind to it.

5. I feel that you're entitled to do whatever you see fit as long as you face the consequences.

6. I think people expect too much of me.

7. I feel that if your drinking (drug use) doesn't hurt other people, it's nobody's business but yours.

8. My main reason for giving up alcohol (drugs) is to make someone else happy.

9. I doubt that very many people give up alcohol (drugs) permanently. I suspect most of them cheat from time to time.

10. I am not an alcoholic (addict).

11. People don't understand the pressure I live with.

12. You can't pass judgment on me unless you've walked a mile in my shoes.

13. If I thought something I did upset other people, I would probably conceal it from them.

14. I am not powerless over alcohol (drugs).

15. I can see myself drinking or using drugs again in the future.

Look at the box below for an interpretation of the results.

Just two positive responses places you at high risk, three or more places you in the "red zone." In either case, complete the exercises at the end of this chapter, and discuss them with your counselor or sponsor.

HOW THE TRAP CLOSES

Two hidden assumptions act as a spring. You begin by convincing yourself that the only thing wrong with drinking or drug use is the problems it causes. You move naturally to a second assumption that the only valid reason for sobriety is to avoid these particular problems. It isn't much of a leap to the conclusion that if problems can be eliminated, minimized, or controlled, relapse is acceptable.

From that point on, your reasoning follows these lines:

The first decision: You decide that for one reason or another, you "need" to return to alcohol and drugs, if only temporarily. Sample rationalizations: you're exhausted, your life is intolerable, you don't get any respect.

Resulting behavior: Almost without realizing it, you begin to examine your life for ways to relapse while containing or minimizing the consequences.

The second decision: You realize the danger of going on a binge, so you may need to find a "protector"—someone to carry out your duties while you are out of control.

Resulting behavior: You cultivate primary enablers—spouse, children, parent, friend, physician, attorney, employer, or combination of above, who can help you.

The third decision: You realize that this enabler must believe his
or her role is actually to "help" you—that it may contribute
to eventual recovery if enabler is patient enough.

Resulting behavior: You may cultivate images of helplessness,
fragility, emotional strain, or extreme dependence, so as to
reinforce enabling and make it difficult for your enabler to
change behavior without feeling guilty and anxious about
outcome.

The fourth decision: You decide to test your new support system by
relapsing.

Resulting behavior: Binge. If enablers manage affairs and binge
does not have too many damaging consequences, pattern is
set.

RED FLAGS

Here is some of the self-talk characteristic of this trap:

1. "I'm not really hurting anyone but myself."
2. "I'm not really damaging myself, either . . . I can handle the
   problems myself."
3. "Sure, I still fall off the wagon occasionally. But I'm doing
   the best I can. I'm making progress."
4. "People wouldn't understand."
5. "I don't have any other choice."
6. "I'll go mad if I don't let off steam occasionally."

CO-DEPENDENT ROLE IN THIS TRAP

It's virtually impossible to maintain this pattern without the
support of a co-dependent. Periodicity—alternating strict abstinence with episodes of drinking or drug use—normally results in increasingly severe binges. During the binge, the addict

is largely out of control. He may drink or use drugs around the clock, stop paying bills, fail to show up for work, run up enormous debts, become physically debilitated, experience a seizure or hallucinations, even get thrown in jail.

Somebody has to be there to pick up the pieces. There must be a *rescuer.*

Co-dependents of addicts in this pattern are often in what is known as the control stage (see "The Twelfth Trap: Family Feud," beginning on page 255, for an explanation of the four stages). In essence, they've given up on the idea of sobriety, and settled for minimizing the adverse consequences of the disease. Rather than seeing themselves as part of the problem (the "safety net" for binges and uncontrolled drinking), the co-dependent views himself or herself as a loving, loyal helpmate— as perhaps all that stands between that addict and death.

Thus the key to changing this pattern is to alter the behavior of the people around the addict. Once enabling is eliminated, the disease itself will push the alcoholic toward sobriety. But that is often a painful struggle for the co-dependent. If enablers were good at watching addicts suffer, they wouldn't have become enablers in the first place.

HOW TO AVOID THIS TRAP

The real question is, Why would someone go to the trouble of entering treatment only to relapse deliberately? Because they believe they are able to control the consequences of addiction.

The Myth of Control Over Consequences

Addicts and alcoholics become control freaks. That's because they have a disease that undermines their control. The worse the disease gets, the more they try to retain control through manipulating people and circumstances.

One option: if you can't drink or use drugs whenever you want, you can at least arrange things to permit an occasional binge.

The following three things will make it easier to binge:

1. Get someone to assist you. When you're on a binge, you're pretty much out of control. Who will take care of the necessities of life while you're awash at sea? You'll need to recruit someone to help protect you from the consequences of your own behavior.

2. Find a safe way to recuperate. Since you become quite ill as a result of these binges, you'll need a method for alleviating the pain and avoiding serious damage. A doctor, or a hospital, for example. Someone you can count on to be there when you need them.

3. Come up with a good excuse. You believe that people will be less willing to help you if they know your intention is to continue doing something that you're aware is bad for you. To ensure their cooperation, you'll have to convince them that you really want to stay away from alcohol or drugs, but something is preventing you. A bad marriage, perhaps. A childhood trauma. Stress from an intolerable schedule. Depression. Unresolved grief over a long-ago tragedy. Whatever seems to be acceptable to the people on whom you depend most. A sales tip: the best excuses are the ones you yourself can believe. That makes them much more convincing to others. Be sure to take advantage of your natural tendency toward denial.

Once you've taken these steps, you're ready to become a chronic relapser. It helps if between relapses you're able to function at an exceptionally high level; that makes it easier for you and those around you to rationalize your occasional slips. You're ready for a life of "managing" the disease.

Of course, that's an illusion. You're not really managing your addiction at all. It's managing you.

Who's in charge here? From our perspective, it's always the addiction. Even if it isn't obvious, addictive disease is still dictating what you can and can't do. Once upon a time, it permitted you to use alcohol or drugs for fun, for "recreation." Then it made you dependent on them, so that you had to use them every so often, or suffer from craving, anxiety, nervousness, irritability. Then it caused you to increase the dose, simply by making smaller amounts ineffective. You weren't worried; after all, you'd always been able to consume a lot without getting intoxicated. But then the disease took that away, as well. You began going on binges, doing things you regretted for reasons you couldn't explain. No matter why you started, it was as though the addiction took hold and shook you until it was finished, leaving you exhausted, depressed, wrung out emotionally and physically. You managed to get off the drug for a while, but you couldn't seem to be happy without it. So you tried to have a little bit and then stop. You couldn't. Now, at last, you reach an uneasy compromise with the illness: you'll arrange things so that you have the maximum chance of surviving what you know will happen when you try a bit of the drug. And hope for the best.

Some "control," huh? But that's what alcoholics and addicts call it. Sometimes they even think that people in AA or NA envy their "freedom." They don't. It isn't really freedom. It's slavery with a longer rope.

EXERCISES FOR AVOIDING THIS TRAP

Exercise One: Self-Diagnosis

Write an essay entitled "How I Control My Life." Discuss the various ways in which you can drink or use drugs without suffering. Give examples from your experience. Then write a second essay called "How I Don't Control My Life." Discuss the various ways in which alcohol and drugs have brought about suffering to yourself or others. Discuss both essays with your counselor or sponsor.

Exercise Two: Attitude Analysis

Below we've reproduced Attitude Check #11, which you completed earlier. Look at the first question.

1. I believe that everyone needs to blow off steam from time to time, myself included.

Sit back and turn on your brain TV. Picture yourself on the screen at the moment before you began your last binge. How were you feeling before you started drinking or using again? Were you "blowing off steam"? Watch yourself on the screen for a few minutes, remembering that experience. Then turn off the set.

Write out a description of your drinking in terms of "steam release." Is that a principle reason for your drinking or drug use? Do you think this is a good reason for drinking or drug use?

Now repeat the process with the second statement.

2. I think most people would consider me a workaholic.

If you agreed with this statement, picture yourself at work. Ask yourself: Why do I work so hard? What am I trying to accomplish? Who am I trying to impress? Do you think people who work really hard deserve to go on a toot every so often? Think it's justified? Write your response.

Continue this process for every statement to which you previously responded positively. Picture the implications of that particular belief on your drinking or drug use. We've provided some leading questions. Consider them carefully.

When finished, go over your responses with a counselor or sponsor. Does your attitude seem to set you up for future relapses? Discuss at some length.

3. I'm a very dynamic person. When I do something, I tend to do it all the way.

Does that mean you believe extra effort justifies falling off the wagon every so often?

4. I believe that you can do whatever you want if you put your mind to it.

Does that mean you believe you can control the outcome of a binge?

5. I feel that you're entitled to do whatever you see fit as long as you face the consequences.

Does that mean it's okay to kill somebody in a car wreck if you're willing to go to prison?

6. I think people expect too much of me.

Does that justify resentments that fuel drinking or drug use?

7. I feel that if your drinking (drug use) doesn't hurt other people, it's nobody's business but yours.

Do you really believe your drinking or drug use isn't hurting other people?

8. My main reason for giving up alcohol (drugs) is to make someone else happy.

What are you going to do if that person gets hit by a truck? Get loaded?

9. I doubt that very many people give up alcohol (drugs) permanently. I suspect most of them cheat from time to time.

Does this mean you feel cheating is okay?

10. I am not an alcoholic (addict).

Do you therefore plan to drink or use drugs?

11. People don't understand the pressure I live with.

Is that an excuse for relapse in your mind?

12. You can't pass judgment on me unless you've walked a mile in my shoes.

Does that mean no one can comment on your drinking or drug use?

13. If I thought something I did upset other people, I would probably conceal it from them.

What about a relapse? A "slip"?

14. I am not powerless over alcohol (drugs).

Does that mean you're going to attempt to control them again?

15. I can see myself drinking or using drugs again in the future.

Then, why aren't you doing it now? What would happen?

Exercise Three: Being Honest

If you've got a secret—in other words, if you're planning on relapsing at some point—follow these steps:

1. Find someone who knows something about alcoholism or drug dependency—somebody at a Twelve Step group, for example—yet who has *absolutely no* personal knowledge of you and no ability to use the information against you. A complete stranger, for example, at a meeting you normally don't attend.

2. Sit down with them and explain your reasoning. Tell them why you plan to drink or use drugs and how you believe you can control the outcome.

3. Ask for their opinion. Take notes on their feedback.

4. Do steps 1 to 3 with four different people, recording each opinion.

5. Read it over before you take the first drink or drug.

THE TWELFTH TRAP: FAMILY FEUD

"When I quit drinking, nobody knew how to relate to me. My dad was still furious, my mom tried to keep everything calm, my sister acted like a watchdog, my brothers avoided me. The counselors said we'd be a happy family again. And I was thinking, When were we ever a happy family in the first place?"

—Recovering addict, age 19

Families are often more committed to the idea of treatment than the addict or alcoholic is. After all, they suffer as much from the disease. A wise man once said that drinking is a solution for the alcoholic, but a problem for the people who have to put up with him.

Commitment to recovery isn't enough. Families often develop habits and patterns that unwittingly interfere with recovery. In fact, some families encourage relapse.

If you're in recovery, the response you get from your family depends in large part on the particular *stage* they happened to be in when you entered treatment.

That's right: like alcoholics, families go through several distinct phases in their response to developing addiction:

STAGE ONE: IN THE DARK

Like mushrooms, addictions grow in the darkness. For a period of months, years, even decades, the family lives with and suffers from alcoholism or drug dependency without recognizing the illness. They attribute many of its symptoms to other causes (stress at work, a "phase" of adolescence, et cetera) and ignore the rest. The longer the alcoholic is able to "function," the harder it is for the family to identify alcoholism. With more virulent forms of addiction (to crack or heroin, for example), the span of blindness is much shorter. The end of this stage is brought about by increasing problems.

STAGE TWO: NEGOTIATING WITH THE DISEASE

The family normally addresses addiction as a behavior problem instead of as an illness. Accordingly, they set out to "fix" it themselves. Because alcoholism is stigmatized, they usually avoid professional help, preferring to rely on their own resources. As their struggle to control drinking or drug use becomes more frantic, they develop a false face to present to the rest of the world—serene, in control, without conflict—but underneath the surface, war escalates.

This is the genesis for many of the behaviors that later come back to haunt the recovery process. The hallmark of this stage is *enabling:* behavior on the part of others that protects the addict from the consequences of drinking or drug use. Classic examples:

Nagging, begging, or pleading

Manipulating social situations to minimize the risk of a "scene"

Monitoring consumption

Efforts to avoid "upsetting" addict

Looking for a "good woman (or man)" to whom to marry the addict off (a favorite of parents)

Sending addict to military school, faraway relatives, distant college

Making excuses to friends, other family members

Paying rent, attorney's fees, or bail for the addict

None of these work. Eventually, the disease reaches the point in its natural progression where the family is unable to keep the problem from spilling over into the outside world. That provides the transition to the third stage.

STAGE THREE: OPEN HOSTILITY

The hallmark of this conflict-ridden stage is *provoking:* behavior on the part of family members that directly encourages drinking or drug use by the addict.

All-out fights over episodes of intoxication

Threats to separate or divorce

Moving out for brief periods to teach the alcoholic a lesson

Throwing the addict out of the house for brief periods and then
  relenting

Taking charge of the checkbook or financial resources

Assuming the addict's responsibilities around the house or
  within the family

Refusing sex

Refusing to speak with the addict

If all goes according to the book, the family members
eventually realize the futility of their own efforts and seek
outside advice. At first, with unerring accuracy, they consult
the wrong people: family friends or neighbors who know even
less than they do. After a while, they stumble on someone who
knows something about alcoholism, and at long last the intervention process begins.

Suppose, however, the addict *doesn't* enter treatment. The
family sometimes leaves. If they don't—i.e., they don't believe
in divorce—they naturally proceed into the next stage.

STAGE FOUR: OVERT CONTROL

Here, the family has given up hope of getting the addict into a
treatment program. They're simply trying to minimize the
negative impact of the disease by managing its symptoms. They
arrange things so that they may live their lives around the
addict, maintaining whatever type of relationship best suits
their needs. When the drinking or drug use threatens, they
reflexively distance themselves until the worst passes. Emotionally, they are detached from the alcoholic or addict. Their
primary goal is to keep the addiction from hurting them. Their
unspoken agenda—so hidden that even they sometimes are

unaware of it—is simply to make their lives as comfortable as possible until the alcoholic or addict leaves or dies.

Now imagine a situation where some members of a family are still in stage one while others are in stages two, three, or four. Suppose the alcoholic decides to enter a treatment program. Here's how they might respond:

If they're in the first stage: They'll be baffled. You'll overhear comments like these:

"Really? Treatment? I didn't even know you had a problem."

"Well, I always knew he drank, but I never thought . . ."

"I think you're so brave to face up to a problem like that."

If they're in the second stage: They still see it as a behavior problem. There will be a tendency to return to enabling and you'll hear comments along these lines:

"I want you to let me know if there's anything I can do to help, just anything at all."

"Are you sure it was really that bad?"

"I think willpower is the key, don't you?"

"Well, can you still go to parties and have fun?"

"When you were in treatment, did you find out why you drink?"

If they're in the third stage: There will probably be some suspiciousness and lingering resentment. After all, they've been living in a battle zone. There will be comments like these:

"I'll give you one more chance."

"You're harder to get along with now than when you were drinking."

"What are you planning to do about your other problems now
    that you're off alcohol (drugs)?"

"You can't expect me to forgive you just like that."

If they're in the fourth stage: They don't believe in treatment;
they believe in relapse. They will be extremely reluctant to give
you responsibilities until you've "proven yourself" for an extended period. You might hear these typical comments:

"What guarantee do we have that you won't fall off the wagon?"

"Don't expect me to forget what's happened before."

"I'm just going to wait and see."

Now, how do *you* respond to their responses? Are you
surprised, disappointed, angry, frustrated, confused? That's
how you fall into this trap.

ATTITUDE CHECK #12: FAMILY FEUD

Let's take a look at your attitudes toward and expectations of
your family. Answer yes or no to the following statements:

1. I feel that once I made the commitment to sobriety, every-
    thing that happened in the past should be forgotten.
2. I plan to rely on my family as my main support for sobriety.
3. I think my family is still angry with me.
4. I'm fortunate that my drinking (drug use) has done little
    damage to others in my family.
5. I believe that my family supports me totally in recovery.
6. I worry that our family will not stay together.
7. I have longstanding conflicts with certain people in my
    immediate family.

8. I feel certain people in my family just want to control me.
9. I feel certain members of my family are partially responsible for my drug (alcohol) problem.
10. I am willing to try to stay sober if my family will agree to support me in every way they can.

Then see the box below for an interpretation of your responses.

If you answered "yes" to two or less of the questions your chance of relapse is low. If you answered "yes" to between three and five of the questions your chance of relapse is moderate and you should continue to learn, and be aware of, the pitfalls of recovery. If you answered "yes" to between six and eight of the questions you are at high risk for relapse and should pay particular attention to this trap. If you answered "yes" to nine or more of the questions you are in a relapse "red zone" and need to seek and follow good advice immediately.

HOW THE TRAP CLOSES

Turn on your brain television for a moment. Imagine yourself coming out of a treatment program after a fairly difficult detox. You're emotionally augmented. You sleep poorly and have nightmares. You get depressed too easily and your moods go up and down like a yo-yo. You forget things thirty minutes after you read them and you're afraid you won't be able to hack it on the job. Your overriding goal is to keep the stress in your life to an absolute minimum. *If I can just get through today,* you remind yourself, *maybe things will seem better tomorrow.* It's like a little prayer.

Done? Okay, clear the screen. Now, visualize a "concerned person"—somebody in your family. Got that? Picture them in an emotionally fragile state. Picture them going to family meetings and trying to read the literature on alcoholism. Imagine how they feel. Don't they seem scared, mistrustful, still angry about things that happened in the past? The relief this person felt when you went for help was replaced within twenty-four hours by an overwhelming sense of anxiety. *What if it doesn't work?* he or she thinks a hundred times a day. *What am I going to do?*

Now, turn off the brain TV for a few minutes and reflect on how your family is reacting to you in recovery.

Perhaps they're still troubled by the extent of your own resentment. *I know it's a disease,* they think, *but some of the things I can't forgive. . . .* Going to the family meetings, attending Al-Anon, reading the literature—it all reminds them of the months and years of sacrifice, taking care of *his* needs, trying to make *him* comfortable, receiving nothing in return but contempt . . .

Maybe when you look at them, you see anger, hurt, obligation, demand. When they look at you, what do you think they see?

Put this combination together, and what do you get? The risk of conflict in a variety of forms:

Firefight

Everyone goes their separate ways until something comes up that requires cooperation. A decision about money, for example, or parenting. A social event that one family member doesn't want to attend. They make a superficial attempt at negotiating a solution, but tempers rise at the first hint of disagreement. An argument ensues, escalating until something really hurtful is said or done. Both sides retreat to their respective allies (other family members, friends, et cetera) to lick their wounds and receive sympathy. Twenty-four hours later, everything is "fine" on the surface. Until the next issue comes up.

Pitched Battle

A state of open war between two or more members of the family. It may be husband and wife, parent and child, child and child, parent and child against child, parent and child against parent. The battle lines usually existed *before* the alcoholic entered treatment, and the treatment experience, it turns out, was only a temporary truce. Divorce or separation is frequently discussed, and the fact that it hasn't taken place already is usually blamed on financial or legal necessities. There is little pretense at reconciliation, and the level of stress is chronically high.

Cold War

Once again, family members go their own ways, preserving an air of superficial calm and togetherness, which masks conflict from the prying eyes of friends and neighbors. Arguments are avoided in favor of a more passive form of aggression: provoking guilt, holding onto unspoken resentments, cultivating an air of martyrdom, criticizing one another to other family members, withholding sex or affection. Some couples even fight with the thermostat—if she turns it up, he turns it down, and vice versa.

Any and all of these provide fertile ground for relapse. The weapons with which family members make war on one another—anger, blame, disapproval, emotional distance—are those most likely to stir up augmented emotions and make recovery virtually impossible.

The irony is that even in the heat of conflict, the family is probably hoping the alcoholic won't relapse. Yet their actions are designed to get them exactly the result they least want— more drinking and drug use.

The first decision: The addict decides that he or she wants to restore their role and reestablish importance within the family system.

Resulting behavior: Attempts to resume duties and privileges in such a way that it provokes resistance from other members—some of whom may have longstanding resentments and/or addictive or psychological problems of their own.

The second decision: Interprets their resistance as unwillingness to forgive past transgressions (which it often is) or as an attempt on their part to maintain control over addict.

Resulting behavior: Responds defensively or aggressively; conflict ensues and continues to escalate.

The third decision: Struggles to understand source of conflict, but is unable to, largely because of interference from augmented emotions; decides that normal family relations are probably impossible.

Resulting behavior: Two options:

1. Sets position in "defense" mode; armors self against real and imagined criticism; rejects responsibility for conflict; battle lines drawn; war begins.
2. Internalizes family anger; cycle of deepening shame and remorse follows; depressive thinking appears; retreats from others and becomes isolative; symptoms of depression proliferate.

The fourth decision: Concludes that sobriety is no longer worth the effort. By this point, has switched focus from recovery to family problems and is no longer able to make clear decisions.

Resulting behavior: Introduces drug; relapse.

RED FLAGS

Watch out if you find phrases like these creeping into your thinking or your family's conversation:

1. "I can't stand this . . . no one could put up with this kind of environment sober."
2. "She's always on my back. We got along better when I was drunk."
3. "Now that I've done what they wanted—got off drugs—you'd think they would appreciate me more."
4. "In some ways, he was nicer when he was drinking."
5. "I just can't forget everything that happened. I'd leave if I could, but it would kill her (him)."
6. "I can't leave because of the kids."
7. "I can't leave because of our financial problems."
8. "I can't leave because I'm still in therapy."
9. "I was thinking . . . maybe I'll just go along with it till the kids are older. I don't think counseling would help. I'll just endure it, as awful as it is."
10. "I've been seeing someone else on the side. I feel horribly guilty, but I don't know what else to do."

RELAPSE IN ACTION

"Ward Cleaver"

Let's take a look at one alcoholic struggling to deal with the family he imagined would be his greatest support.

Once upon a time there lived a man who believed that his family was about as good as a family could get. His name was Ward Cleaver.

No, that wasn't really his name. It was just a little joke. He was always talking about the importance of a family and pretty soon his buddies took to calling him Ward Cleaver and it stuck. He actually liked it, because he meant every corny word.

Maybe that was partly because his own childhood hadn't been happy. His father left them and died of liver cirrhosis a decade later. Of all the achievements in his life, he was most proud of his family.

Like most parents, he mentally held his breath when his eldest son reached adolescence. Nevertheless, he was completely unprepared for the trouble that ultimately befell. In Ward's eldest son's school locker—we'll call him Ned—the principal had found a small amount of a substance that looked suspiciously like crack, a notebook of dates with initials beside them, two beepers, and a neck chain of multiple thick ropes of high-quality gold.

Last but not least, they found a beat-up Adidas shoebox with $3,200 in twenty- and fifty-dollar bills.

At his lawyer's recommendation, Ward took the boy for evaluation and treatment. After the first few sessions, Ned's counselor called for a family meeting. The therapist informed Ward and his wife that Ned's major complaint was his father's alcoholism. Ward's shock was further increased by his wife's strong agreement. Before the end of the session (and to his own surprise), Ward had agreed to see his physician for further evaluation. His second major shock came when the doctor told him he was an alcoholic, and sent him off to the Betty Ford Clinic for a month. He put up a fuss but everybody kept reminding him that he'd promised (*stupid! stupid!*) he would do whatever the doctor recommended.

Surprisingly, he didn't mind the program all that much. He especially liked the opportunity to attend chapel, because he'd always felt secretly bad about his lapsed church attendance. Ward didn't really believe in God, but he had great faith in regular church attendance as a pillar of the American family. He concluded that church attendance was going to be a big part of the family's immediate future.

So when he left the program he chose a Sunday evening to reveal his new plan to the entire family.

He gathered them all around after dinner. Somehow this didn't seem like the same family he'd left to go to the treatment center. His eldest son had turned into a man, seemingly overnight. Then there was his younger son, David, who'd been invisible through the recent turmoil. *When did he start wearing his baseball cap backwards? It makes him look like a moron.*

These revelations spurred Ward's commitment to bring religion back into the family. It wasn't only a good idea—it was a necessity!

He passed out stapled copies of something, one for his wife and one for each son. "It's a schedule," Ward said. "I'm suggesting we set aside every Sunday as Family Day, dedicated to doing things as a family. We go to the early service at eight o'clock. In the evening we can sit around and read the Bible or talk about ourselves and our feelings before we go to bed."

He waited for a response. Nobody said anything for several minutes.

"This is a crock of shit," Ned said. "You go away for a month and then come home and start telling us what to do. What gives you the right?"

"I'm your father, and don't you forget it!" Ward thundered. "As long as you're in my house, you'll do what I tell you!"

"Every time I turn around, it seems like somebody is telling me what to do," Ned shouted back. "You people can't get your own act together, so you take it out on us!"

Ward was homicidal. "Ned, if you breathe so much as one more word, I am going to knock you across this room." And he meant it.

"Okay, fuck it, I'll get the hell out of here," Ned hissed. And he stalked out of the house, slamming the door on his father's angry voice and his mother's weeping.

Ward sat down in his chair and put his head in his hands. His wife just sat and cried. "This is your fault," she said. "You never listen to anybody but yourself."

Then everyone sat without speaking for what felt like hours but must have been five or ten minutes. Eventually David, the youngest member of the family, broke the silence. "Can I watch TV?" he said.

Later, Ward realized those were the first words he'd heard the boy say all day.

A few hours later, Ward was sitting by himself in the den pretending to watch a Jack Nicklaus videotape on the ideal putting stroke. His wife had gone to bed. Ned had not reappeared, and Ward wondered whether they would see him again tonight. At the moment, Ward himself was visualizing a glass of whiskey with three perfect cubes of ice.

He heard David come into the room.

"David," he said. "Do you mind if we talk for just a second?"

The boy shrugged.

"Why is Ned so angry with me? Was I that bad a father? I don't remember yelling at him or anything."

The boy looked embarrassed. "I didn't say that, Dad. It's just that . . . you kind of have to be Ned to understand it."

Ward shook his head. "All those evenings just kind of blur together."

"That's real hard to believe, Dad, that you don't remember things. I just figured we weren't that important to you."

Ward felt the tears again. "You're the most important thing in my life."

David frowned as he spoke. He seemed to be thinking out

loud. "It's like sometimes you were there, and sometimes you weren't . . . you'd go into the den after dinner and sit and drink and fall asleep, and nobody could wake you."

"This is unbelievable," Ward said.

David seemed to think his father was questioning his veracity. "No. It really happened, Dad. I wouldn't lie about something like that. Like that TV show where the guy puts on these headphones and travels to other planets. Meanwhile his body is just sitting in a chair in his living room on Earth." The boy stopped, puzzled by his father's expression. "Maybe you didn't see that show."

Indeed, Ward was traveling back through time at that very moment. Back to when he himself was David's age, coming home from school to find his father passed out on the couch at four o'clock in the afternoon, the stink of whiskey and cigarettes all over the house like a toxic cloud. He remembered how that felt. How he felt. How much he hated his father, with every fiber of his being.

And how much, he understood at last, his own sons must hate him.

"Son," he said slowly. "I'm so sorry." He felt the tears well again.

David seemed surprised at the apology. "Oh, it wasn't that bad, Dad. Ned just takes things too seriously."

After that, the conversation seemed to run out of gas. David turned on the TV. Ward couldn't think of what to do with himself. Finally he decided to go for a drive. *Maybe that will clear my head,* he told himself.

By this time, Ward was in the grip of an epiphany of sorts. He was coming to see, for the first time in his life, that the priests had been right: there existed sins of *omission* that were as damaging as those you committed. He was beginning to understand how neglect was really as bad as outright assault; how letting people down—especially people who loved you and depended on you and counted on you to be there for them—was about as bad as taking a stick and beating them to the ground.

Ward was overwhelmed with the feeling of remorse. *It's all my fault,* he told himself. *It's time I took responsibility for it. At AA, they talk about rigorous honesty. Facing up to what you are—even if you're a miserable SOB.*

He stared at the oncoming headlights, thought about how easy it would be to swerve over into the traffic, imagined the impact, the sweet sleep that would follow . . . Suddenly, he broke into a cold sweat and sat up straight in the seat. *What are you doing?* he thought in a panic.

There was an exit looming on the right. He pulled into an all-night minimart. He was suddenly ravenous. *I haven't had a chili dog since I was in college,* he thought. He bought two, added a big bag of corn chips, a pack of Twinkies, a six-pack of light beer. Driving off, he thumbed through stations until he found a talk show where they were discussing some woman's experience being abducted by aliens and taken to another solar system.

Ward chewed happily on chili dog between gulps of beer. *Listen, sister, you think you got problems . . .* he thought as he listened to her on the radio.

The next thing Ward knew, he was being helped out of his car. Someone in a white uniform was urging him to lie on a stretcher of some sort, and there was a cop car with lights whirling and a cop standing in the open door, talking to someone on a radio and looking suspicious. Which was when the whole thing came clear in his thinking, for the first time. *I've really done it this time.*

Even his cloudy mind could see the irony. *Now I've had a drunk-driving arrest,* he thought. *I always said I'd know I was an alcoholic if I ever got arrested, and now I have been . . .*

HOW TO AVOID THIS TRAP

Start with the following simple steps:

Step One: Recognize first of all that there is more than one "sick" person in the family. Whatever you've told yourself about your drinking not affecting the people who love you is probably fantasy. It will be a long time before either you or they fully appreciate what happened within your family as a result of prolonged exposure to this disease.

Step Two: Make a list of the problems you are currently experiencing in your relationship. Describe each one with examples. Sometimes it helps to make use of your brain TV; simply visualize a situation on the screen and play it through. Watch how you relate to other people, and how they respond to you. This is to clarify your own thinking.

Step Three: Seek guidance from a professional who specializes in addictions and family treatment. Describe your situation and ask for feedback on the source of the problems you are experiencing.

Step Four: With the professional's help, arrange a session that includes the other members of your family. Discuss the issues that you and the professional decided were important. Listen to the feedback you get from your family members. Ask the professional to make recommendations to you *as a family* regarding what you might do to alleviate existing problems and forestall future ones.

Step Five: If the professional identifies any of your family members as in need of treatment or individual counseling, support this.

Step Six: Encourage your family members to attend Al-Anon or Alateen and to read books about the illness and recovery. Answer questions they might have as honestly as you can.

Step Seven: If you feel yourself getting unusually emotional in some interaction—angry, remorseful, et cetera—take a break and do something else to lower the level of emotion. Then discuss the issue with your counselor or sponsor before bringing it up again with your family member.

Step Eight: Remember: your primary goal is to *maintain perspective*.

There are no perfect solutions. After all, there are others involved, and they have their own problems. And we all know you can't control other people.

RESOURCES

THE
TWELVE STEPS
OF
ALCOHOLICS
ANONYMOUS

1. We admitted we were powerless over alcohol—that our lives had become unmanageable.
2. Came to believe that a Power greater than ourselves could restore us to sanity.
3. Made a decision to turn our will and our lives over to the care of God *as we understood Him.*
4. Made a searching and fearless moral inventory of ourselves.
5. Admitted to God, to ourselves and to another human being the exact nature of our wrongs.

6. Were entirely ready to have God remove all these defects of character.

7. Humbly asked Him to remove our shortcomings.

8. Made a list of all persons we had harmed, and became willing to make amends to them all.

9. Made direct amends to such people wherever possible, except when to do so would injure them or others.

10. Continued to take personal inventory and when we were wrong promptly admitted it.

11. Sought through prayer and meditation to improve our conscious contact with God, *as we understood Him,* praying only for knowledge of His will for us and the power to carry that out.

12. Having had a spiritual awakening as the result of these steps, we tried to carry this message to alcoholics, and to practice these principles in all our affairs.

Reprinted with permission of AA World Services, Inc.

APPENDIX: EXERCISES WITH MODELS OF ADDICTION

Exercise A

Prepare a history (either written or recorded into a tape recorder) of your experience with people who had alcohol or drug problems. Describe your relationship with each and your feelings about that person's drinking or drug use. Include stories you heard from your parents or other adults about the hopelessness of alcoholism. Then write the answer to the following question: "Why Do I Believe Addicts Can't Stay Sober?" Once that's done, share it with a counselor or sponsor. Talk about your experiences. Did you "over-identify" with someone who relapsed or died of alcoholism?

Exercise B

Make a list of the important people in your life. Include your parents and other adults who were around when you were a child. Beside each name, write briefly (where you can) that person's attitude toward alcohol or drugs. If possible, include something they said about an alcoholic or addict, or about drugs themselves. Then discuss with a counselor or sponsor. Were any of the significant people in your life strongly opposed to alcohol or drugs on the grounds that it was wrong to drink or use drugs?

Exercise C

Make a list of the important people in your life. Include your parents and other adults who were around when you were a child. Beside each name, write briefly (where you can) that person's attitude toward alcohol or drugs. If possible, include something they said about an alcoholic or addict, or about drugs themselves. Then discuss with a counselor or sponsor. Were any of the people on your list strong believers in self-discipline or self-control, especially in regards to drinking? Did you try to emulate them?

Exercise D

Make a list of the medical and health professionals who have talked with you about alcohol or drugs: doctors, nurses, health educators, teachers, et cetera. Include films you may have seen (and books or articles you may have read) on the subject. Can you recall anyone saying that alcoholism was "self-induced"? That once an alcoholic regained his health he could return to controlled drinking? Discuss with a counselor or sponsor. What are the weaknesses in this view? Does it hold true for most alcoholics?

Exercise E

Make a list of the AA or NA members with whom you have become close, had an ongoing relationship, or who make a particular impression on you. Did you hear something at AA or NA that seemed to contradict the view that alcoholism/addiction was a disease? If so, what? Discuss with a counselor or sponsor.

Exercise F

Make a list of the following: (1) psychiatric or mental health professionals with whom you have discussed addiction; (2) books or articles you have read about the psychology of alcoholism and drug dependence; (3) discussions with significant people in your life about why people drink or use drugs. Try to recall the conversation—what attitudes were expressed? How did they influence you? Discuss with your counselor or sponsor. What is wrong with the idea that your drinking or drug use is a symptom of an underlying problem?

Exercise G

Make a list of books or articles you have read that portray alcoholism and drug addiction as learned behaviors. What did you find attractive about that view? Compare it to the idea that alcoholism is a disease. What in your view are the relative strengths and weaknesses of each? Discuss with a counselor or sponsor.

Exercise H

Compare the family systems model with a chronic disease model. What in your view are the relative strengths and weaknesses of each? Make a complete list. Then discuss with a counselor or sponsor.

GLOSSARY

Addictive Disease: A category of chronic, progressive, and potentially fatal diseases involving the ingestion of drugs or alcohol.

Alcoholism: An addictive disease characterized by the ingestion of alcohol and featuring a variety of symptoms including tolerance, withdrawal, organ deterioration, compulsion, loss of control, and continued use despite adverse consequences.

Blackout: A period of time when drinking, which the drinker cannot recall when sober.

Cocaine (or Stimulant) Addiction: An addictive disease characterized by the ingestion of cocaine or other stimulants and featuring craving, compulsion, loss of control, and continued use despite adverse consequences.

Compulsion: A strong drive to continue using a drug.

Continued Use Despite Adverse Consequences: A symptom of addiction; the addict continues consumption in the face of mounting problems.

Craving: A persistent, recurring desire for a drug, often in the form of vivid dreams, intrusive thoughts, euphoric memories, or acute hunger.

Loss of Control: Another symptom of addiction, springing from compulsion and characterized by three behaviors: The user consumes more of the drug than intended; consumes the drug at times or in places where it puts him at risk; or consumes the drug for extended periods (binges) without stopping.

Narcotics Addiction: An addictive disease characterized by ingestion of narcotics and by tolerance, physical dependence, craving, compulsion, loss of control, and continued use despite adverse consequences.

Organ Deterioration: Measurable damage (through medical examination) to the liver or other organs due to excessive consumption of alcohol or drugs.

Sedative Addiction: An addictive disease featuring ingestion of sedatives and hypnotics and characterized by tolerance, dependence, loss of control, and continued use despite adverse consequences.

Tolerance: The ability to consume larger than expected amounts of a drug without obvious signs of intoxication.

Withdrawal: Signs of physical and psychological discomfort when a drug is withdrawn.

SUGGESTED READING

There are so many books about addiction that we can't possibly include them all. Here are a few of note.

Alcoholism

Under the Influence, James Milam, Ph.D., and Katherine Ketcham. Bantam Books, 1984.
Probably the best general guide to alcoholism as a disease ever written. Required reading for every alcoholic and family.

Alcoholism: The Genetic Inheritance, Kathleen Whalen Fitzgerald. Doubleday, 1988.
Updates some of the information in Milam's work. A thoughtful, well-written book.

Alternative Diets:

The Self Healing Cookbook, Kristina Turner. Earthtones Press, Box 2341-B, Grass Valley, Ca.

The scientific evidence isn't persuasive, but several clinicians we know claim success in alleviating some of the mood swing and somatic discomfort of early sobriety through a macrobiotic diet. If you want to try it, this is the book of choice.

Cocaine Addiction

800–Cocaine, Mark Gold, M.D. Bantam Books, 1984.

Brief and designed for the layman. Includes an excellent self-test for addiction, with explanations of various symptoms.

Treatment

Don't Help: A Guide to Working with the Alcoholic, Ronald Rogers and Chandler Scott McMillin. Bantam Books, 1988.

How to treat alcoholism and drug dependency from the standpoint of a chronic disease rather than a moral or psychological problem. Includes a discussion of how to overcome denial through a series of exercises.

Recovering, L. Ann Mueller, M.D., and Katherine Ketcham. Bantam Books, 1987.

A basic review of the disease, treatment, and recovery for alcoholics and their families. Easy to read and understand, yet comprehensive.

Relapse Prevention

Counseling for Relapse Prevention and *Staying Sober: A Guide for Relapse Prevention,* Terence Gorski and Merlene Miller. Herald House; Independence Press, 1986.

Two very good introductions to the issue of relapse from the perspective of treating a chronic disease. The first book is aimed at counselors and the second at the recovering person. Gorski was among the first to approach relapse prevention in any systematic way, and his work is used in many modern treatment programs.

Family

Getting Them Sober, Parts One and Two, Toby Rice Drews. Bridge Publishing, 1980.

Good, practical advice for the family member, in contrast to many other books on this subject. Teaches the co-dependent how to become part of the solution instead of the problem.

Freeing Someone You Love From Alcohol and Other Drugs, Ronald Rogers and Chandler Scott McMillin. Price, Stern, Sloan Publishers, 1989.

A comprehensive guide to intervention, treatment, and recovery for family members of alcoholics and addicts. Includes a chapter on how to get someone who has relapsed back into treatment.

Intervention

Intervention: How to Help Those Who Don't Want Help, Vernon Johnson. Johnson Institute Press, 1986.

Includes examples of confrontation sessions. Little discussion of dealing with the relapsed alcoholic.

Living on the Edge, Katherine Ketcham and Ginny Lyford Gustafson. Bantam Books, 1989.

An introductory discussion of enabling and intervention. Again, does not devote much attention to intervening with the addict who has already been through treatment and relapsed.

Twelve-Step Programs

The Twelve Steps Revisited, Ronald Rogers and Chandler Scott McMillin. Bantam Books, 1988.

How does the alcoholic reconcile the medical reality of the disease of alcoholism with the spiritual program of Alcoholics Anonymous? That's the focus of this book.

Living With Chronic Medical Problems

We Are Not Alone: Learning to Live With Chronic Illness, Sefra Kobrin Pitzele. Workman Publishing, 1989.

A cheerful and practical guide to dealing with chronic ailments such as arthritis, diabetes, heart disease, and lung ailments. You'll see many similarities to recovery from alcoholism.

Living With Psychiatric Problems

The Good News About Depression (1988) and *The Good News About Anxiety* (1989), Mark Gold, M.D., Bantam Books.

Believe it or not, there are even fewer useful books about mental illness than about addiction. These are two exceptions: practical, well-written, and helpful to the layman.

Surviving Schizophrenia: A Family Manual, E. Fuller Torrey, M.D. Harper and Row, 1988.

Torrey is to the treatment of schizophrenia what Milam has been to alcoholism: a clear voice in a vast wilderness. An essential guide for anyone whose family has been afflicted by this disease.

Publications of Alcoholics Anonymous and Narcotics Anonymous

Alcoholics Anonymous, Bill W. and others, 1955.

The "bible" of AA. Includes the all-important chapter, "How It Works."

Twelve Steps and Twelve Traditions, Bill W., 1953.

The "official" interpretation of the Steps and Traditions of AA.

Living Sober, 1975.

Practical advice for the first days of recovery.

Narcotics Anonymous, 1982.

NA's version of AA's Big Book.

Nutrition in Recovery

Eating Right to Live Sober, L. Ann Mueller, M.D., and Katherine Ketcham. NAL, 1986.

Nutrition and diet for the recovering alcoholic. Probably the most medically authoritative of the numerous books on the importance of diet in recovery.

Exercise in Recovery

Staying Sober, Judy Myers, Ph.D., with Maribeth Mellin. Simon and Schuster, 1988.

A recovering alcoholic tells her story and gives practical advice about exercise and diet for recovering persons.

ACKNOWLEDGMENTS

We must acknowledge all those whose help was invaluable in the preparation of this book: Phillip Lief, Lee Ann Chearneyi, Julia Banks, Linda Loewenthal, Maria Mack, and our agent and friend Bob Markel.

We would also like to thank Benjamin Westheimer, a pioneer in the use of guided imagery in education, who taught us the technique that later became "brain television." And as always we acknowledge our debt to James Milam whose biogenic paradigm has once again guided us through the myths and misconceptions that surround addiction.

ABOUT THE AUTHORS

RONALD L. ROGERS is a clinician who has directed numerous addiction treatment programs and is currently a consultant for New Beginnings in Warwick, Maryland.

CHANDLER SCOTT MCMILLIN is director of the Addiction Treatment Center at Suburban Hospital, one of the largest in Washington, D.C.

Together, they have also co-authored four previous books: *Don't Help*, *The Healing Bond*, *The Twelve Steps Revisited*, and *Freeing Someone You Love from Alcohol and Other Drugs*.